Blessings

SONDRA DANKEL

ISBN: 1482093871
ISBN 13: 9781482093872

MEET THE TURNERS

CONTENTS

DEDICATION

This book is dedicated to my parents. God "blessed" me with wonderful parents. Life was not easy for them. My mother was adopted and my father grew up poor on a farm. In spite of hardships my parents taught their three children to worship God, the love of country, respect for our elders, compassion for animals, and willingness to help people less fortunate than ourselves.

Children, obey your parents in the Lord, for this is right.
"Honor your father and mother"—
Which is the first commandment with a promise—
That it may go well with you and that you may enjoy long life on the earth.

Ephesians 6: 1-3 (NIV)

PREFACE

Christmas is approaching, and this is Kim Turner's favorite time of the year. Of course, it is hectic with four children. This is baby Kevin's first Christmas. Kim reflects on being a woman, a mother, a wife, a sister, and a daughter. She always thanks God for his many blessings of good health, happy children, a loving husband, a forever friend in her sister, and caring parents.

Kim lovingly watches her children as they grow. Parents are not perfect, and we sometimes learn as we go along. She makes their house "a home" and the people within it are truly a family. They really care about one another's feelings, and handle each one with love. Sometimes understanding is not easy, but Kim and Howard pray for patience and guidance in raising their family. They know that the saying, "A family that prays together stays together," is for real.

Blessings—we have so many to be thankful for, Kim muses as she thinks about her family. She feels blessed every time she sees little Kevin's smile or hears Susan's sweet singing. Katie is transforming from a teenager into a woman, and Andrew is just growing too fast. Spending time with family is precious. Life is too short to be bitter or nasty. Kim believes if there is a problem, the family should talk about it, resolve it, and go forward, because we can never go back.

Remember yesterday is history
Tomorrow is a mystery
But today is a gift.

By Alice Morse Earle

We cannot change what happened yesterday,
Nor can we see into tomorrow, so
We must live today to the fullest.

INTRODUCTION

Blessings is the first in what I hope to be a series of books about the Turner family: parents Howard and Kim, daughters Katie and Susan, and sons Andrew and Kevin.

The Turner family has two pets: Kit-Kat the cat and Midnight the dog. The Turners live on Deerwood Drive in Skippack, New Hampshire.

I hope *Blessings* will be the beginning of an exciting journey. Many of the places in this book are real, but Skippack is a fictional town, just as the Turners are my fictional family. In writing about them, they have become quite real to me—but just in the book, of course.

I believe *every woman*, whether young or old, will smile and find love and laughter between these pages. Maybe sometimes you will even relate to the situations the Turners encounter. I hope you will invite the Turners into your home, and that you enjoy *Blessings* so much that you will look forward to book two.

BLESSINGS

CHAPTER 1

Events are always happening in Skippack; even in the schools. They have programs, plays, and musicals. With four children, Howard and I stay very busy. When we moved here we had two children and thought our family was complete, but God decided otherwise. My OB-GYN doctor told me I could not conceive again, because I had some medical problems that would prevent me from ever getting pregnant again. He is no longer my OB-GYN doctor! When we thought we were all done with crying babies, dirty diapers, and potty-training, I became pregnant with our third child, a little girl. Our oldest was eight years old and our youngest was almost six. Then five years later, we had a baby boy. At the time, they were a shock to us, but not a mistake. They are both blessings from heaven, and were conceived in love.

God is good.

As I walked across our family room, I looked at our oldest daughter, Katie, who just turned fourteen going on twenty-four. She thinks she has all the answers. She is developing into a lovely, young lady. She has graceful, beautiful features. Her long dark hair frames her face, and all you can see are her big brown eyes and long eye eyelashes. She is thin and tall, and boys are starting to call. "Lord, help me is a quick prayer that goes through my mind every day." I often imagine her as a ballerina. However, she is not interested in ballet. Actually, she has a good head on her shoulders, and we have taught her right from wrong. We all attend church on Sundays, and Katie belongs to a Christian youth group. She has made many nice friends. She was such a good little girl; she behaved well, and I always knew where she was at all times.

Then, came Andrew. Talk about opposites in the same family. Andrew is now eleven and cannot wait to be thirteen, a teenager. He is already interested in cars—not girls, which I guess is a good thing. He likes sports and plays on the school's soccer team. He is my adventurous one, the daredevil, the one you cannot hold down. I am sure he will give me all of my gray hairs. Of course, his mission in life is to tease and torment his sisters. He is a loving child, though, and I would not want him any other way. His grandparents remark that his blonde hair seems to reflect a halo. A halo? I must put brighter light bulbs in the living room lamps!

The first one of our "newer babies" is Susan. She is six years old and a tom-boy, but then again, she is also the mothering, nurturing type. She is a little home-body. She wants to take care of everyone. She is so cute. She has freckles and light reddish-brown hair that seems to glow in the sun light. She loves to pick out her clothes to wear. Sometimes, quite often, I have to intervene. She is not only the informant, but also, the inquisitive one. She asks questions all day long: Where did he go? Who is she? Why must I do that? When can I have candy? Are we there yet? Why?"

Last is our newest little angel, Kevin. He is only nine months and a very good baby. He just, on his own, stood up in his crib for the first time today. Before we know it; he will be walking. Something happens when they start walking. It seems their arms grow very long, and if something is not within their reach; they will figure out a way to get what they want. I remember Andrew at nine months. I walked into the kitchen and saw that he had a pull toy with a box on top of it, and he was trying to climb these in order to get a cookie from the counter. Thank goodness I got to him quickly before he fell. Children are amazing. Never under-estimate what a child may try to do!

The November days were flying by and the excitement of Christmas and the holidays was quickly approaching. The autumn air is brisk. I think it clears our minds and prepares us for the cold winter ahead. We watched the Veterans/Armistice Day parade. This day is to celebrate and honor patriotism, love of country, and willingness to serve and sacrifice for the common good. Every year, we make an effort to attend this parade as a family. We respect our men and women in uniform. I think how these veterans survived in times of warfare, and yet they have taught us good morals and values, and have shown us what is right and wrong. For some of us, these veterans also taught us to pray and read the Bible, and to ask God for direction in our lives and our country. Our country was founded on these religious principles. These principles should not be changed just because some people do not like them. We were taught to show respect to those in authority, and the importance of disciplining our children.

I am busy trying to buy most of my Christmas presents before the Thanksgiving holiday. That way I will have more time to do all the other fun things with the children: shopping, decorating, school programs, and whatever else comes along as we prepare for Christmas. I want to get most of the food and things we need for the Thanksgiving dinner, too. Shopping the day or two before the holiday is just crazy, so I try to get as much done as I can ahead of time. A nine-month-old gets cranky after a while, and so do I. Then again, I have to admit he is so much fun to take with me. As I walk through the mall, or in and out of the shops in town and in the supermarket, people comment on how adorable he is, and they try to talk to him. I let him ride the mechanical pony in front of the toy store in the mall, holding him steady, of course. He enjoys that. Usually in the afternoon, he falls asleep in his stroller. I do not shop at the mall often because it is too far to travel and to park there is a headache. I prefer to shop locally in town. Sometimes his Mom-Mom babysits for me. It is a blessing that she lives so close to us.

I have to hide the presents before the children come home from school. I hide them in my bedroom closet until they are wrapped, and then they go into the attic behind a hidden door that the children do not know is there. Thank goodness we have a separate small freezer and another refrigerator/freezer in the basement. Our kitchen refrigerator/freezer just will not hold everything. In addition, with a large family, I try to buy things in bulk or on sale.

I have sent my husband to the store a few times to help me. God bless us! What was I thinking? I try to keep it to very few times. The phone rings constantly while he is shopping, with him calling me to ask, "Where do they keep the raisins? Where is the flour? Do we really need four boxes of cereal? Do I have to buy sanitary napkins for our daughter?" He drives me crazy! Then he gets angry standing in the checkout line. The person in front of him doesn't have enough money to pay for their order, or the cashier calls out, "We need a price check here!" By the time he gets home with the groceries, he is not pleasant to be with at all. Gee, I do not return home that miserable from grocery shopping.

"We eat too much!" He says loudly. "We should all be on diets! That store drove me nuts!"

"Thank you honey; did you find everything on the list?" I ask this so sweetly I could choke.

He rolls his big brown eyes at me and I think I hear a growl. "Here is your list, and yes, I bought everything," he says. "Kim, I am going to sit down for a while and drink a soda."

"Ok, thank you, dear," I said. I had to chuckle to myself. He only telephoned six (or was it seven?) times from the supermarket. Men in grocery stores—not the place they want to be.

In a few short weeks, it will be Thanksgiving. The children are home, and everyone in the neighborhood and in town is decorating for Christmas. On Thanksgiving, there is an early church service that we attend from nine to ten o'clock in the morning, and then it is football and dinner, but no parade. The parade is saved for the Fourth of July. Thanksgiving is when the women cook and the men fall asleep.

Susan, our six-year-old daughter, came to me in the kitchen and said, "Mommy, our teacher said this is a holiday, and it is wonderful cause no one has to go to school or work." I am thinking her teacher is Miss Brooks, and she is probably going to her mommy and daddy's for dinner and carrying a store-bought pie with her!

A woman's work is never done. After I have done the cleaning, the cooking, and all the laundry, I often tell my family jokingly, "Do not touch anything, eat anything, or dare to change your clothes, because it will only mean work for me. Keep your coats on, don't change your clothes, and let's go out to eat!"

But not today; today is Thanksgiving, a special day.

Looking at our sweet little girl, I just said, "Yes, dear," as I kept *working* on the stuffing for the turkey. My husband's mother will be here soon to help me finish preparing everything. My sister and father will not be traveling to spend this holiday with us, but we look forward to their visit this Christmas. Today they will be enjoying dinner with church friends. Thanksgiving is the busiest travel time of the year, and it is not wise to come all this distance. I think it better that they stay home where it is safer.

Little do the children know that they will be helping on this day. We just will not call it *working*. They are certainly old enough to help wash dishes, dry dishes, and put things away. Of course, we always package food for our company to take home.

I am not a drinker, but I do like a glass of special wine with a holiday dinner. We buy the non-alcoholic wine, and the taste is delicious. If I were to drink some real wine right now, I just might forget to stuff the turkey!

I have a magnet on the refrigerator with the saying, *I cook with wine; sometimes I even put it in the food!*

I am glad we are not a drinking family. I tell our teenage daughter that if you need to drink to have fun, there is a problem. People's personalities change when they have too much to drink. A drunk can change quickly from being a wonderful person to being someone you do not want to be near. You cannot reason or argue with a drunk. He is right, and you are wrong. Everything is his way or no way.

I look at my menu for today to make sure everything has been prepared. We will have more than enough food to eat. Our guests are bringing the pies and whipped cream. Howard's mom is making the sweet potato casserole and the green bean casserole. I do not think we will starve. We may gain weight, though. When I think about all this food, it almost makes me feel guilty preparing it.

Yesterday afternoon my oldest daughter, Katie, and I made Thanksgiving baskets at the church to donate to needy families. We really enjoyed it and had fun conversing with the other church members. A few ladies cooked hot dogs and chili, and brought desserts. We paid for that lunch, and the money will go directly to the church kitchen fund. Last night my husband and older son delivered the baskets. It makes you feel good to help others so that they can have a wonderful meal too. In this great country, no one should go hungry. It is sad and almost unbelievable that many people do. It is even twice as sad when you realize it just may be folks in your community, and you were unaware of their needs.

An older couple who is new to our church, Jonathan and Beverly Cooper, will be joining us for dinner this year. They moved here from New York State a few months ago and are still settling into the neighborhood and church. They are very nice, so we welcomed them to our home for the holiday.

I heard the doorbell ring. "I'll get it," screamed Andrew, our oldest son. I washed my hands and entered the living room.

"Hi, there," I said. "I am sorry Andrew hollered so loudly," I added as I gave him a look. "Welcome, and come in. Here's Howard; he will take your coats," I said as my husband walked into the living room to greet our guests.

"Hi, all," said Mr. Cooper. "We wanted to bring you a little thank-you gift, so we brought you a basket of fruit. We figured with your large family, it would certainly be eaten."

"Oh, you didn't have to do that," Howard and I both said almost simultaneously, and then I added, "but thank you."

"Let me help you with your baked items, Mrs. Cooper," I said.

"Please, call me Beverly, and my husband, Jonathan," she said.

"Good, thank you," I answered. "You know us by Mr. and Mrs. Turner, but our names are Howard and Kimberly. You may call me Kim. Dinner will be ready soon; please help yourselves to some cheese and crackers and some veggies. We have non-alcoholic wines and iced tea to drink. We also have iced water if that is what you prefer."

"Thank you; the food looks delicious," Beverly said.

"I am anxious to know—what kind of pies did you make? They look wonderful," I asked.

"I made pecan and apple," Beverly answered. "They were my mother's recipes, and they are very good, if I do say so myself." We both giggled. "I brought homemade whipped cream too," Beverly said.

"Oh, that is the best," I said. "I can't wait for dessert."

"Grand-moms here!" yelled Susan.

"I guess you know I have arrived," said Margaret as she came through the door. "Boy, it is cold out today. Does the weatherman predict snow?"

"Hi, Mom," Howard said as he gave his mom a kiss on the cheek. "Just a dusting of snow is all we're supposed to get."

"You are my big turkey, but where is my little turkey?" asked Margaret.

"You must mean Kevin," answered Howard. "He is here somewhere with the other children."

When Margaret saw the Coopers, she said, "Hi, I'm Howard's mother. You may remember me from church."

"Oh yes, we certainly do. I am Beverly, and this is my husband, Jonathan."

"My name is Margaret."

"Does anyone ever call you Marge or Peggy?" asked Beverly.

"Sometimes I go by Marge or Margie, but never Peggy," answered Margaret. "I like Peggy, but I just do not see Peggy as a nickname for Margaret," she added.

"Kim's table is set so lovely, and this is a wonderful house," said Beverly. "How does she keep it so neat with four children?"

"Thank you, Beverly," I said, overhearing her compliment. "I have a trivet on the kitchen wall that reads *Our house is clean enough to be healthy and dirty enough to be happy*. With four children and two pets, I cannot take any chances on what the house will look like when company visits. If it is a real mess, I rush to write a get well card, write a note in it to myself, and place it on the television in open view so the visitor will believe I have been ill and not able to clean for a while!" I announced.

"Kim, you are too funny," Beverly said with a laugh.

Earlier in the day, my children had helped me set the table for nine people. Katie and Susan helped me drape the autumn tablecloth with a cutout leaf design, and then we put a set of Thanksgiving salt and pepper shakers on each end of the table, one a pair of turkeys and the other a pair of pilgrims. The centerpiece was a pumpkin surrounded by leaves, flowers, and gourds. Andrew rolled the napkins and put them in the silver napkin rings. Katie set out the place settings and silverware. Susan put the cold foods on the table, such as the olives and pickles. We placed two candles on the table, but we made sure not to set them too close to the centerpiece.

"Kim and Howard are wonderful together. They were perfect for each other right from the beginning," Margaret said to Beverly. "It was love at first sight. In today's world, many marriages do not last long. I hate to admit it, but I am proud of them, and pleased. I am blessed."

"Yes, you should be," said Jonathan. "They seem like a nice couple, and they are trying to raise their children right. Marriage is something you have to work at, but if a couple is truly in love, it shouldn't be difficult."

"It is harder for kids today," said Beverly. "Everything is competitive, there's too much bullying in the schools, and there is no respect or discipline at home. Our world is making the children grow up too quickly. It seems they are not allowed to be children any more. The computers are wonderful, but sometimes the sites the teenagers view are not good for them. Our government never should have taken prayer out of school, either."

"By the way, did you meet all of our children?" I asked the Coopers.

"We don't remember all their names, but we have seen them running in church," Beverly said.

"If they are running, they must be ours," I replied. I called all the children to gather around so that proper introductions could be made.

"This is our oldest daughter, Katie; she is fourteen. Next is Andrew; he is eleven. Susan is our six-year-old, and then we have Kevin, who is nine months old and just learning to crawl. He will be standing soon on his own. We saw him stand once so far."

"That's when your headaches will start," Beverly said, and then she smiled and added, "We are glad to meet all of you."

When we all sat down to dinner, Susan, are youngest daughter, told everyone to fold his or her hands in prayer, because everyone was to say a prayer out loud as to what he or she was thankful for on this special day. She told everyone the prayer had to be short but sweet.

Howard smiled as he prayed first. "Lord, we thank you, not just today but every day, for this family, our friends, our home, and our health, and I thank you for my job."

Next was Jonathan. "Thank you, Lord, for this food and the hands that prepared it."

Beverly said, "Thank you for wonderful neighbors and Christian friends."

Next to speak was Howard's mother. "I am so thankful, dear Lord, for the love my son gives to his wife and family, and for the love he gets in return."

The baby, of course, said, "Da-da-da." Maybe he was saying the first two words of the Lord's Prayer.

Susan was next. "God bless this food, and I hope all the poor people get plenty to eat today. My mommy and sister made baskets for them."

"Thank you for this warm home and all this food," said Andrew.

Katie smiled and spoke next. "Our Father, thank you for my wonderful parents and family. We are glad our friends could join us for dinner today."

I was last. I smiled as I looked around the table. "Thank you for Jesus; thank you for everyone here today, and thank you for everything, even in good times and bad. Amen."

We had an enjoyable day with our new friends. They told us about where they had previously lived in Alfred Station, New York, and how much they missed it. They said their house and property had become too much for them to care for. Alfred Station is in the country. It is a nice area, but they decided they needed something smaller and easier to maintain. They decided to settle here in Skippack. They had always liked coming to New Hampshire on vacation, so why not move here after retirement. They have other friends in this area, too.

"The church people have been very nice to us," said Jonathan.

"The Bauers are super folks, too," said Beverly. "They own the General Store. They seem to know everyone and everything that goes on in this little town. They are so informative, too."

"They are great people," said Howard, "and they are very helpful. Most of the storeowners in Skippack are nice. A few will 'boil your bubble' at times or make you a little angry, but for the most part, there are good people here."

"We love it here," I said. "We looked around before we settled here. Don't you love downtown Skippack with its unique shops and eateries?"

"Sometimes it reminds me of a town from long ago," said Margaret. "It is quaint and charming."

"We agree," said Beverly.

"Kim and I love the Elwood Covered Bridge Gift Shop. Have you been there yet?" asked Margaret.

"No, I haven't," answered Beverly, "but I would love to go there. I heard it was a friendly place to shop, and that they sell really nice things."

"Well, how about I give you a call later next week and the three of us will plan an afternoon to visit there?" I asked.

"That would be fun, Kim, thank you. I will look forward to it," Beverly said.

"Mom, you do want to join us, don't you?" I asked.

"Of course! Me turn down a shopping day? Do I look sick?" Margaret asked.

We just laughed. Margaret is always ready to do anything fun. Just say the word and she is ready to go. "Did you see the pottery in the kitchen with the gray-blue design? That pottery came from there. It is made here in New Hampshire. The children have given me many pieces as gifts," I said.

"The Elwood Covered Bridge Gift Shop is the cutest thing," Margaret said. "They have gifts for every season of the year."

"Mom and I might sell some wreaths to the store. We make seasonal wreaths," said Katie.

"Oh, I would love to see them. I could use one for the front door," remarked Beverly.

"Are you interested in a Christmas wreath now?" asked Katie. "I could go downstairs and bring up a few of our Christmas wreaths for you to pick one."

"Ok, that sounds great," said Beverly, and when the men joined them from the other room, she remarked, "Well, I guess the football game is over. My husband is ready to go home."

I laughed and said, "I know how men are. When the game is over and their stomachs are full, they are ready to go home to bed."

Katie returned with four different Christmas wreaths to show Beverly.

"My goodness, they are all so lovely. You said the two of you make these?" asked Beverly.

"Yes, my mother and I make them downstairs. We hope to sell some on consignment at the covered bridge gift shop, and we will sell them at the church Christmas bazaar next month."

"I thought I saw something in the bulletin about a church bazaar. I always enjoy them," commented Beverly.

"Mark the date on your calendar," I said. "We always have a fun and happy time."

"May I wait and buy one at the bazaar? I really would like to look at the other ones too. You say you have them for all the holidays?"

"Most of the ones we take to the bazaar are for Christmas," I said, "but yes, we have wreaths for all the other holidays."

"Ok, I look forward to it, and I will purchase some wreaths from you at that time."

"Thank you, Beverly," I said as I gave Beverly a hug, and then I shook Jonathan's hand. "We're glad you could join us for dinner. Your pies were delicious."

"Thank you for an enjoyable day and an even better dinner. Your children are delightful," said Beverly.

"The threatening worked!" I laughed.

"You are both gracious hosts," said Jonathan.

"Thank you," Howard replied, and then he said to Margaret, "Are you leaving now, too, Mom?"

"Yes, dear, it is getting late. I will see you tomorrow morning. I will call when I am in the house to let you know I arrived home safely." We always have her call when she gets home. It gives us peace of mind to know she is safe and secure.

Beverly said, "I know your mother-in-law babysits for you, but if there is ever a time she cannot, I would love to babysit for you. Kevin is adorable, as are your other children."

"Thank you, Beverly," I said warmly. "I'll keep that in mind!"

“See you tomorrow, Mom,” Howard and I said to Margaret as we kissed her goodbye. “The casseroles were good, too.”

“Oh, Beverly, before you go—we’ve already told Mom this, but did we mention to you and Jonathan that Howard is being sent to Maui, Hawaii for six days? He leaves tomorrow afternoon. It is for his job, but the exciting part is that I can go with him on this trip. Yippee! I am so excited,” I said as I did a little dance. “Actually, we just found out a few days ago, so we have been packing and getting things set up for Mom and the children. It is crazy! Mom is coming here to stay with the children and, I didn’t think to ask you earlier since I was busy with the meal, but she just may need your help, if that would be okay with you.”

“They go to Hawaii and I stay home,” said Margaret. “That is okay, though, because I will be with all of my grandchildren. Katie will help me, and Kim threatened Andrew to be good, and Sue is like a little mother to Kevin.”

“We leave tomorrow afternoon and return very early on Thursday morning,” I said. “We will be staying at the Royal Lahaina on Ka’anapali Shore.”

“Oh, that is wonderful for the two of you,” remarked Beverly. “Have you ever been to Hawaii before?”

“Yes, we spent our honeymoon there for ten days. It was wonderful and beautiful, and we loved every minute of it.” I said as I smiled at Mom and Beverly.

“I will call you on Saturday, Margaret,” Beverley said, “and I will come over and help you in any way I can. The only plans we really have for this weekend are to visit our other friends and go to church on Sunday.”

"That sounds great. I made sure the freezer and the refrigerator are stocked with food, and there are plenty of leftovers from today. Oh, thank you so much, Mom and Bev; may I call you Bev?" I asked.

"Yes dear, that is fine," answered Bev.

People come into our lives for a reason, a season, or a lifetime.

CHAPTER 2

I usually like to take a number of clothes with me on a trip: something for evening, a sundress, shorts and tops, bathing suits, cover ups, and so on, but this time I tried to be smart and pack only what I thought I would really need. Howard looked like he was moving. Our bedroom was covered in his summer clothes.

"Why do you need all of these clothes?" I asked.

"Well, we can enjoy ourselves on Friday night, Saturday, and Sunday, which means I'll need lots of casual clothes for those days, but for work on Monday and Tuesday, I have to wear a suit and look professional," he answered.

"Ok," I answered. He had everything for every occasion. "Looks like you have covered everything. You have clothes for a funeral, a church service, a wedding, a meeting, a day on the beach, and a night in town. I believe your closet is empty. Maybe you do not need all these things," I added.

"I don't know what I need, but it is going with me just in case I do," he answered.

"You know they charge for extra luggage weight," I commented. "Are you going to wear your clothes in layers on the flight so that your luggage will be lighter?"

"Kim, this is on my company; I'm not worried about the extra charge. Besides, I do not think it will be overweight," Howard explained.

"No, I like my idea better. You can wear it all and gradually peel it off!" I laughed. "You know we can always buy some things there. We are not going to a third world country!" I said. "I am throwing in some fold-up carry-on bags for souvenirs."

My biggest problem will be putting on my bathing suit for the first time this season. All sorts of thoughts whirled through my mind. Have I gained weight? *Is my bathing suit stretched out of shape? Is it ruined from swimming in chlorinated water? Does it have pulls, stains, and tears, and will the straps still hold up a thirty-seven-year-old woman who hopes she looks younger and not like she's had four children?*

And then there was my obvious lack of a suntan. "Look at me, Howard; I am winter white. I will look like Kimmy the Ghost on the beach. I can sit right next to Casper!"

"Tarzan to Jane; listen, honey, you tan beautifully and quickly, and so do I. You will be tan in no time. If you want a new bathing suit, I am sure they sell plenty of them in Lahaina. Would you like me to pick one out for you?" He winked, and I saw that twinkle in his eyes I loved so much.

"No, I am quite capable of picking out my own bathing suit, thank you. You would have me buy one of those little bitty things the teenagers wear; no, thank you."

Howard and I really feel funny leaving our four children at home, because it's been so long since we've been on a vacation alone together, but how often does something like this come along in our lives? A free trip to Maui,

Hawaii, for the two of us—yes, we are excited. Yes, the kids can stay home! That funny feeling left as quickly as it came.

The Rapid Rover van, heading to the airport, pulled into the driveway. We kissed and said our goodbyes as the van's driver started to load our luggage into the back.

"Love you all, thanks Mom, see you at about seven o'clock Thursday morning," we shouted as we got into the van. We were on our way to Boston's Logan Airport. We finally got through the security check and made it to our plane.

We found our seats in the coach/economy section, and settled in for the three-hour flight to Atlanta. We were not on the plane long when we heard a little girl about five years old start to whine. *Ok*, I thought, *her parents will take care of her and she'll quiet down soon*. Then the whines got louder. Someone actually made a comment to the parents. The mother, who acted like a child herself, told us that her daughter probably would fall asleep, but "look out when she wakes up!" At that point, a passenger seated nearby mumbled jokingly, "Give that child some whiskey!"

After the beverages were handed out and the trash was collected, the flight attendant told us to put our seats in the upright position and put up our little trays in preparation for landing. I guess the rude lady in front of me did not hear her. I gently tapped the lady in front of me, but she would not straighten her seat back, so all I saw was the top of her head. But then she lifted her head and turned around to stare at me with a look that said *If I want my seat back, I will keep it that way*. I had to call over the flight attendant and ask her to tell "Miss Sweetness" in front of me to put up her seat.

Before the plane landed, the whiner woke up. The mother was right. I looked to see if there might be anything wrong with this little girl, but I think she was just a terrible whiner and the parents allowed it. Miss Sweetness in front of me lowered her seat back again. I thought of hitting the tray every few minutes to really make her day, but then I decided it might be better to just look at the in-flight magazine and hold it high enough to hide my face in case she turned around and stared at me again. If dirty looks could kill, I believe I would be dead from the last look she gave me. It was easy to see that the louder I flipped the pages of the magazine, the more annoyed she became. Eventually, she sat up. I believe it was the same moment I heard we were circling the Atlanta airport for landing. You want to have a pleasant flight and be cordial to everyone, but some people are just rude.

When the plane landed, we wanted to kiss the ground. We had a layover of an hour and a half. That wasn't too bad. At least we could get something to eat and use the restroom facilities. We then flew to Honolulu, Hawaii, and from there we had a connecting flight to Maui. We were told our flight from Atlanta had been a little late, so we could not fly to Maui for about three hours.

"Oh, come on!" Howard said in frustration when he heard this announcement. "We could swim there quicker!" he hollered. The actual flight to Maui would only take twenty-five minutes, but we had to wait to take that flight.

So we took a walking tour of the airport, including a lovely indoor tropical forest. I bought a couple of leis, put them around our necks, and we kissed. Howard bought a paper to read and I looked at brochures. "We must go to a luau. I read that one is at our hotel. Remember we had so much fun at the one on our honeymoon?" I reminded him.

"Can you believe we have been married for over sixteen years?" Howard asked.

"Did you bring me along to trade me in on a new model?" I countered.

"So you figured it out. Of course; why else would I bring you along?" Howard smiled. "I am glad you could come on this trip with me, Kim. We love our children, but we have to admit this is a great little get-away for us."

"It is, isn't it?" I mused.

"Believe me, Kim, there is no one I would rather be with than you," Howard added, and we kissed.

After landing in Maui, we picked up our rental car. A red convertible was our choice. The ride to our hotel was about a half hour or more. The weather, of course, was beautiful, and we enjoyed riding with the top down. The Royal Lahaina Resort is very nice and the pools are great. This huge hotel is right on the water. Every morning, a breakfast buffet is served out on the terrace. When you are finished breakfast, you leave your plate on the table, but before the waitress can remove it, the birds fly down and partake of any leftovers. We booked a night for a luau and the ride to the Haleakala Volcano Crater to see the sunrise. This is Maui's highest peak. Today we might just hang out at the pool. Maui is known as the "Magic Isle," but we just call it *paradise*.

"Howard, we can walk on the beach at sunset and see the runner with the lighted torch. He runs and lights other torches on his way. Then he climbs on the rocks and dives from the cliff into the water," I said. "Maybe on Monday or Tuesday while you are working I could take the tour on the Road to Hanna. It is an all-day trip. Remember we did that last time we were here?"

"I remember the hairpin turns and no guard rails," said Howard.

"Yes, but you really get to see a different side of the island with the volcanic rocks and black sand beaches. I think I will do it," I said.

Saturday we drove to Lahaina. We love Lahaina. You can buy everything Hawaiian there. It is a fun place to shop and eat. Lahaina is a historic whaling village. It was once the whaling capital of the Pacific. There is one restaurant in town, and if anyone sees a whale out in the ocean, he or she rings the whale-bell.

"Hey, I'm hungry. How about we eat at Bubba Gump's?" suggested Howard.

"Great, I love it," I answered. We sat near an open window and watched the parasails coasting over the water.

"Do you want to try it, Kim?" Howard asked.

"No, I think I will pass. I do like to watch them, though. Are you going to snorkel?"

"I may," said Howard. "We can rent everything for snorkeling at our hotel."

As we were preparing to leave the restaurant, a fellow walked in who looked quite familiar.

"Howard, look—my goodness, he looks just like Tom Hanks in the movie *Forrest Gump*." He was dressed the same and carrying a box of chocolates.

We walked outside just behind him, and he turned around to ask us if we would like to sit on the bus stop bench and have a photo taken with him.

"Oh yes, hi there," we said, and then we introduced ourselves. "We are Kim and Howard Turner from New Hampshire," said Howard.

"Hello to you two; my name is Forrest," he said. He spoke just like Forrest from the movie. He was certainly a double for Tom Hanks. We smiled, and someone took photos of the three of us. It was fun to sit, talk, and laugh with this man. When we got up to walk away, the man said, "Yes, life is like a box of chocolates. You never know what you will get," a quote from the movie. (When we returned home and told this story to our friends, no one else had ever seen this Forrest Gump double at a Bubba Gump restaurant. It was our special memory, and we have the pictures to prove it.)

After our exciting afternoon, Howard bought a Hawaiian shirt and I bought a little dress to wear to the luau Sunday night. Everyone dresses Hawaiian for the luau. If you do not dress the part, you look out of place.

This town has the largest banyan tree. There is much history here. We saw the old mission house and walked the docks behind the Best Western Pioneer Inn, the oldest hotel on the island of Maui. They were having a craft and art show in the park where the large banyan tree stands. We even stopped at a couple yard sales, and we bought stuff, too. "Even though this is a short trip, you know everyone will want a souvenir. How about we give these as Christmas presents since it will be Christmas soon?" I asked Howard.

"Yeah, I agree," he answered. "I think that will be the best thing to do. The kids will hate it, though."

"The kids? You mean your mother!" I exclaimed. "I can hear her now: 'I have to wait until Christmas to get my gift.

I watched their children for almost a week'!" We laughed at the thought of how funny she could be.

"Well, then we will give the gifts to everyone when we get home," Howard said.

"Besides, I know I will be too excited to wait," I commented.

As we browsed in one of the stores in Lahaina, we asked the shop owner about real estate on the island. Of course, real estate in Hawaii is very expensive. The shop owner told us that homeless people were sleeping in the bushes on the beach. I told Howard we'd better hurry and tag a bush, just like we do when we find the right Christmas tree; that way we would have a piece of land for the next time we came back. The shop owner laughed.

The Birds of Paradise flowers are growing everywhere. This tropical flower is unique and the colors of orange and purple are beautiful. Birds of Paradise are my sister's favorite flower. The orchids grow wild here. We saw Hawaiian or perhaps Polynesian women making real flower leis from the fragrant Plumeria tree. We walked the beach and went to bed quite early. We were still tired from the flight.

* * *

Back at home, Margaret was busy supervising the children. On Friday morning, they all wanted to watch television, play their Wii games, or be with their friends. As long as they seemed to behave and not fight, and Margaret knew where they were, everything was ok.

Bev called and asked if she could be of any help to Margaret on Saturday.

Margaret said, "Sure, Bev; I don't know what I'll need you to do, but I am sure you will be of help. Please, come over."

Bev came over on Saturday as promised. She and Margaret were tackling the housework together. "Margaret," Bev asked, "what do the children call you? I think I heard both Mom-Mom and Grandmom when I was there for Thanksgiving."

"I answer to both," Margaret said.

Bev talked to Margaret as she did the laundry, and then Bev said she would run the sweeper downstairs.

"Oh, that would be a great help; thank you," said Margaret. Little did they know what was happening in the upstairs bathroom. Susan and Andrew wanted to surprise everyone by bathing the dog in the bathtub.

"Now you hold her, Andrew, and I will scrub her," said Susan.

"No, you hold her and I will scrub her. You cannot reach over her," said Andrew.

"Yes, I can," shouted Susan, and then she laughed. "Look at all the bubbles!"

"You were supposed to use dog shampoo, not bubble bath," yelled Andrew. "Rinse her more. Hey, you are getting the floor all wet!"

"It's your fault!" hollered Susan.

"Let's dry her off now," said Andrew. "We need lots of towels. We cannot let her run wet through the house or Mom-Mom will have a fit."

"Maybe I should get the hair dryer and her brush, and I could brush her when she dries," said Susan.

"No, don't open the door or she will...," and before Andrew could finish his sentence, Midnight bolted out the door and through the upstairs shaking all the way. Down the stairs she ran. Margaret said she thought her eyes would just about pop out of her head when she saw the expression on Bev's face.

"Oh, help! What was that?" screamed Bev as Midnight shook water everywhere. Bubbles were bouncing off the dog and dropping onto the rug and furniture. Beverly toppled backward into a chair.

Margaret stomped up the stairs. She could hear water running and the kids saying, "We better clean up fast or she will be mad."

"Too late!" Margaret said as she opened the bathroom door. "Look at this place! Towels are on the floor, the rugs are soaked, you've splashed water and suds on everything, and there is dog hair everywhere! Who told you both to wash the dog?" Andrew and Susan just stood there in silence. Margaret continued. "To begin with, why didn't you ask to wash her in the downstairs bathroom? That way she would be near to the basement door and the upstairs would not be covered in water and dog hair."

"We wanted to surprise you," Andrew said meekly.

"Well, you did."

"When I went to get her brush, she got out, Grandmom," said Susan.

"Yes, I saw that," Margaret said. "Poor Beverly downstairs is still in a state of shock. She was not expecting a large, wet dog to be running through the house."

"We're sorry," they both said.

"Ok, we have some cleaning to do in here, and you are both helping. First, please go downstairs and apologize to Mrs. Cooper."

After they left, Margaret had to laugh. *Kids—you never know what they will do!* she mused.

Thinking of the kids reminded her that she had no idea where baby Kevin was at that moment. Margaret raced down the stairs and asked Bev, "Where is Kevin?"

"I thought he was with Katie. I will look for him," Bev said as she walked into the kitchen. The floor had just been vacuumed and mopped. In the one corner of the kitchen the dog dishes sit in the dog dish tray. There was Kevin, covered in dog food and splashing in the water bowl. "Well, are we having fun yet?" Bev said as she laughed. Then she spotted Kevin crawling toward Midnight. "Oh, my, look at this little boy! It looks like he tried to eat some of the dog food, too. Somebody needs a bath."

Margaret came into the kitchen and said, "Let's see what Katie is doing. Perhaps she can give Kevin a bubble bath and he can play in the water. Did Susan and Andrew apologize for scaring you half to death with the wet dog? I hope you did not hurt your back falling into the chair."

"Yes, they did, and no, I didn't. They are comical; each blames the other. They are typical brother and sister."

"Oh, yes, that is an everyday thing," answered Margaret. "Either they blame each other or that invisible person known as 'I don't know who did it'."

Katie came around the kitchen door. "Look at you," she laughed when she saw Kevin. "No wonder Midnight had that 'deer in the headlights' look—someone was trying to eat her dog food. By the way, the dog is all wet."

"I am not going to worry about it unless Kevin starts to bark," Margaret said. "He doesn't seem to be choking, so I assume he is fine. Katie, would you give him a bath, please, and then he can have some lunch and hopefully take his nap. You will have to use the downstairs bathroom. I want to check on the two house-wreckers upstairs."

"I am almost afraid to ask," Katie said, and she smiled knowingly. "What did they do?"

"They decided to give Midnight a bath with bubble bath," remarked Margaret. "What a mess!"

Katie tried not to laugh, but when she heard them arguing upstairs, she couldn't hold it in any longer.

"Thank you for helping me today," Margaret said to Bev. "I am sure you will not offer again. I have to admit it—the look on your face when you saw that dog was hilarious!" The two women just stood there and laughed. "Your eyes were big and your face was completely white. You were so funny," Margaret giggled.

"Of course, I will come here any time you need me. I love children. We were not able to have our own children and we never adopted any, but we fostered a few children years back. I have to admit they were good children, and I believe we sent them on the right road. You feel so bad for foster kids. Life should not be that way for them," remarked Bev, but wanting to keep the mood light, she changed the subject. "This really is a nice house. I love the way Kim decorates. The color combinations really complement each room. It is a fairly large house to keep clean, though," she added. Turning to Margaret, Bev announced, "You will have to walk down the street to our house to visit us sometime. Our house is a rancher. I wanted everything on one floor. I will have you, Kim, and the baby for lunch someday soon."

"That would be nice," said Margaret. "I would like that. Maybe we can do that the day we go to the Elwood Covered Bridge Gift Shop?"

"That would be great," was Bev's reply.

* * *

Howard and I had to be at our meeting place at two o'clock in the morning. Everyone looked more like going back to bed than embarking on an hour-and-a-half ride in a minivan to the top of the Haleakala Volcano Crater to see the sunrise. It amazes me that people actually ride bicycles halfway up and down this mountain. Maybe Howard could do it, but not me. There are no guardrails along the sides of the road, and sometimes cattle are on the road, even after dark. Hairpin turns along the way make the drive challenging, too. Halfway up there is a rest stop with bathroom facilities. Thank you, Lord!

Almost everyone went back to sleep the minute the door shut to the minivan. I did not want to awaken anyone, so I whispered to Howard, "If I ever think about trying to ride a bike up here, just take me to a shrink, because you'll know I have lost my mind! If I did try it, the halfway stop is where I would be pronounced dead! Then again, I probably would have died a long time before that, and my body would have been dragged behind my bike to the halfway stop. Yes, that would be my last breath and last turn of the pedal."

Howard just shook his head and chuckled quietly. I took that as encouragement and continued with the dramatic retelling of my tragic demise. "Engraved on my tombstone will be the words, *Devoted wife, good mother, loving daughter, faithful sister, and just plain stupid! What was she thinking?* They never say how many people do not make it, die from peddling, or fall off the mountain, do they, Howard?"

Howard commented with a little laugh, "The halfway stop is where you start, uphill."

The bicyclists are driven in minivans to the rest area, and they ride their bikes from there up and then back down. It is a sight to see the bicyclists as they ride back and forth in a single line up and down this mountain. In the daylight, the view is great.

When you reach the top, you just try to keep warm and comfortable as you wait for the sun to rise; it usually takes about an hour or so. It is very dark when you arrive, but as the sun gradually rises, the clouds disperse, and it gets a little brighter. It is amazing to see so many people there enjoying the experience with you.

The perfect photo is when the sun rises enough so that you have a bright display like a starry sun. It is something you do not want to miss as a tourist. You only have a moment or two to get this photo, and then the opportunity is gone. It is magnificent to be able to capture this moment of sunrise. People come here from around the world to witness this display of the sun. They set up their tripods and camera equipment to get the perfect shot. We had to dress in warm clothes, because in the early morning hours before dawn, it is quite cold up here. Howard's entire wardrobe came in handy, as I wore most of it: a T-shirt, sweatshirt, hoodie sweatshirt, sweatpants, socks, and another T-shirt. It's hard to imagine that we will probably be swimming this afternoon. As the sun rises, so does the temperature. By the time we return to the bottom of the mountain, the temperature will be in the high seventies or low eighties, and it will still be early morning. On the way down, we will stop for breakfast with the others on our tour.

⋆ ⋆ ⋆

At home in New Hampshire, it is Sunday, and everyone was getting ready to go to church. Kevin did not want to leave the cat, as the cat wanted to sit under his highchair while he dropped his breakfast to the floor, bit by bit. "You think that is funny, Kevin?" Margaret said. "You will be hungry when we come home." Kevin seemed a little miserable this morning. "Oh my, little one," she said as she lifted him from the highchair, "I think either you miss Mommy and Daddy or your teeth are bothering you. Mom-Mom will kiss you and make you all better."

"Katie, what is that you have on for church?" Margaret asked. "I see it is an outfit, but it is shorts and a jacket. Your legs will be cold."

"Oh no, Grand-mom, I will be fine," she replied. "The shorts are really warm."

"Are you wearing tights under them to keep your legs warm?" Margaret asked.

"Yes, Mom-Mom."

"Ok, but I really do not like to see you wearing shorts to church." Turning toward the stairs, Margaret called out, "Susan, Andrew, are you ready for church?" Both came down the stairs. "Andrew, you look alright, but tuck in the shirt and wear a belt. Susan, did Katie help you get dressed?"

"A little," she answered.

"You look nice in that dress, but fasten your dress shoes and bring your comb and brush to quickly do your hair. Hurry, it is getting late," Margaret told her.

Margaret held Kevin so that he could stand in the pew. He smiled and made faces at everyone sitting behind them. Howard and Kim did not know, but their little boy had just learned how to say amen. Whenever the pastor paused in his sermon, Kevin yelled out, "Amen!" Pastor Johnstone laughed and made the comment, "I do not remember asking for audience participation, but I am glad someone is listening to my sermon." After the congregation sang a hymn, Kevin clapped his hands as he scanned the room looking to see whose attention he could get. Children learn quickly!

The weather became really ugly in the afternoon. Margaret told the children she wanted them to stay home since the roads were icy, and it was cold and windy, too.

Kit-Kat, the cat, likes to sit in the window seat and watch the birds and the leaves fluttering in the trees. He is comical. It is so windy today that every time the wind blows the leaves, he ducks behind the windowsill. Then, a second later, he pops up his head. When he watches the birds, his tail wags and he makes a cackling sound with his mouth. When the birds fly to another tree, he jumps from one window to the other. Maybe he thinks he can fly too. Windy days keep him entertained.

"I have an idea," said Margaret to Katie and Susan. "Why don't we make dinner together? I am sure I could use the help. How about lasagna? Katie, you can help me with that, and Susan, you can make the dessert. What would you like for dessert?"

"I know what we could have that we haven't had it in a long time," Andrew said as he entered the kitchen.

"What is that, dear?" Margaret asked.

"A chocolate cream pie," said Andrew.

"Would everyone like a chocolate cream pie for dessert?" she asked.

Margaret heard a unanimous yes. "Ok, Susan, I will help you with the pie. Andrew, your job is to put your brother down for a nap, and then you can set the table. This is a family affair." The children seemed to enjoy this, and dinner and dessert were fun. Some of the other meals they had were not so much fun. The baby vomited, Susan didn't like that kind of syrup, the kids were kicking each other under the table, Andrew wanted French toast and not pancakes, Katie didn't like the oatmeal—all accompanied by nonstop chatter, such as "He's touching me," "Katie is staring at me," or "Grand-mom, you say grace today."

Margaret would just say to herself inwardly, *Do I scream first and then say grace, or do I say grace first and then scream? Maybe a time out will help; that is what I need!*

⋆ ⋆ ⋆

On Sunday, Howard and I visited the little Ka'ahumanu Church in Wailuku. We had attended a church service here sixteen years ago when we were on our honeymoon. The minister greeted us and asked us to stay for refreshments after the service. We accepted his invitation. The church people were so nice. Some ladies were wearing their traditional dress. We really felt blessed to come to this wonderful old church again. Howard and I laughed and said that now we have twice the wonderful memories.

We enjoyed spending time at the pool all afternoon. In the evening, we had a great time at the luau. The people at a luau are fun. Some get up on the stage and try to learn the hula, and others just eat, sit, and drink. Everyone is happy, the music is loud, and the night is beautiful.

"You look like one of those Hawaiian girls," Howard said. "Will you dance to the Hawaiian wedding song?"

"Unfortunately, no, but I do love when the girls dance to that song. It is quite beautiful to watch. Remember this from our honeymoon? By the way, did you check out the orchid earrings I bought to complement my dress?"

"Oh yes, I did see them. You look very pretty. You even have flowers in your hair." Howard smiled.

"Well, I like the shirt you are wearing. I like the little huts and canoes on it," I said. Then we both laughed.

Howard had to work on Monday and Tuesday. I decided to lie around the pool in the morning and then go into Lahaina to shop in the afternoon. I bought chocolate covered macadamia nuts—so good—and Hawaiian coffee. I decided to buy Katie some Hawaiian jewelry, Susan a summer dress, Kevin a little shorts set, Andrew a Hawaiian coconut head, and Mom a book about Maui and a piece of jewelry. For Howard and myself I bought photo albums to hold our pictures of this trip. Tonight I will sign up for the Road to Hanna tour.

As I made my way to the parking attendant, I could see vendors lined up outside the hotel. *Oh goody, I can shop here too. All I have to tell Howard is, "I am a woman and that's what women do best!"* There were handmade Christmas ornaments. The Hawaiian way to say Merry Christmas is

"Mele Kalikimaka," so of course I had to buy one of those ornaments. There were beautiful crafts, many with dolphin designs, and lovely jewelry items for sale. I love dolphins, so I purchased a little of this and a little of that.

When Howard comes back to the hotel, we will take a swim and have a nice dinner. We have to eat seafood tonight. My mouth is watering for some. It seems like I cannot get enough of it. Wednesday we have to leave this lovely place. I am enjoying the papaya for breakfast, the warm breezes, and the gorgeous flowers. Howard took a picture of me with hibiscus flowers in my hair. We walked in the evening holding hands, just like we did on our honeymoon. We took pictures of the sunset so that now we will have photos of both the sunrise and the sunset in Hawaii.

On Tuesday evening, we were invited by the concierge of the hotel to a cocktail party on the terrace. It was wonderful. There were assorted beverages and appetizers. I actually wore a short dress and high heels. Howard wore none other than a Hawaiian shirt.

"You look very lovely, lady; do you come here often?" Howard asked.

"No, but I certainly would like too," I answered him, and after a moment's pause, I said, "I love and miss our family, but do we really have to go?"

"Yes, I am afraid so," he said as he kissed me. "Do you think my mom could just move in with us permanently?"

"She is probably ready to pull her hair out by now," I said, "but at least every time we called there were no horror stories, so I guess things are ok at home!"

* * *

The children went back to school on Monday. The roads were still icy, and there were many accidents. Margaret was relieved when the last child came through the door after school.

"Your parents will be home Thursday morning before you leave for school," Margaret said. After saying that, she thought she should not have mentioned it, because they would either not want to go to school that day, or they would dawdle while getting ready and be very late. Oh well, too late; she'd told them now. "I guess you all can't wait to see what they bring home for you. Let's have the house clean and all the laundry done because they will be tired from the flight, and they will have their own laundry to do when they arrive home. So tonight let's get the work done, and maybe tomorrow night we can play with the Wii or watch movies. Make sure you do your homework, too."

As the older ones did their homework and some cleaning, Margaret decided to give Kevin his bubble bath. He had a great time splashing and playing with his little boat and rubber ducky.

"Ok, my little guy, it is time for bed," Margaret said. "Mom-Mom will rock you a little and sing to you, and you can go to sleep, my sweet." Margaret left the water in the tub, as she planned to return later to clean the bathroom. There were still many bubbles in the water. While she was putting on Kevin's pajamas, she heard *splash* and a loud meow erupted from the cat. Everyone came running to the bathroom to see what happened. Kit-Kat must have been batting at the bubbles in the tub and had fallen in, but he had jumped out of the water just as quickly. There in the hallway outside the bathroom was Kit-Kat. Everyone was hysterical with laughter. He looked so frightened, but funny. He looked like someone had taken gel to his hair and made points sticking out all over his head and body.

His eyes looked so big. He took off down the hall and into the parents' bedroom. Three children were not far behind. Water and bubbles were everywhere. Margaret just shook her head and mused, *First the dog, and now the cat. It is a rerun of Saturday. Well, at least the pets are clean. Maybe we should start shutting the bathroom door, or maybe we should let the water out of the tub immediately. Oh, help! If it is not the kids doing something, it is the animals.*

The bed in the parents' room is king sized, and of course, Kit-Kat had decided to hide under it in the very center. The three children were giggling as they tried from both sides of the bed to retrieve the scared cat.

"I have him," shouted Katie. "Oh, you poor thing; you are trembling, and are so wet. Grand-mom, I will take him to our room and dry him off, and hopefully he will calm down. That was so funny!"

"I want to come with you, Katie," said Susan.

"Ok, that's fine," said Margaret. "Andrew, I'm sorry, but you are the one left to help me clean. Would you please wipe down the hallway and bathroom? I will be there soon to finish with you. Let me get little Kevin to bed first."

"It's ok, Grand-mom," answered Andrew. "Kit-Kat looked so funny. We should have taken a picture. I can't wait to tell Mom and Dad. He looked just like that scared cat with the big eyes on those greeting cards."

"Oh, yes, I remember those funny cards, too," Margaret said.

* * *

Howard and I had three flights home. The first took us to San Francisco, the second to Chicago, and the third brought us back to Boston. The first flight was good, and during the second flight, we both tried to read or sleep. I don't even remember what movie was available, but it sounded so awful. On the flight from Chicago, we sat directly behind the first class section. Someday before I die, I want to sit in first class. I want to say, "I'm rich; wait on me."

The curtain that separates first class and coach really annoys me. Just once I want to get up and throw open that curtain and say, "Ah-hah, I caught you!" I got up to use the restroom just behind the wall we were staring at, and when I opened the door, the flight attendant came over to me.

"I am sorry, but this bathroom is for first class passengers only," she told me.

I said, "What? I can touch this restroom with my hand. My seat is facing this wall. It is right here and available."

She told me I had to use the restrooms in the back of the plane.

"You mean I have to go all the way back there when the bathroom is right here?" I asked.

"Yes, I am sorry, but those are the rules," she said.

I sat down again and looked at Howard and he just shook his head. "I feel like Rosa Parks on the bus," I said to him. “Do I do this differently? I think I will write a letter to this airline when we get home. I am not happy about this.” Little did I know it, but the situation was about to get worse.

I walked to the back of the plane to use the restroom. I could not even see the actual back of the plane from our seats—that's how far forward we were. I had always heard that on long flights you should try to get up and move around a little so that your legs do not cramp and blood clots do not form in them. Tell the flight attendants that. They don't mind you getting up and using the facilities, but then they want you back in your seat as soon as possible.

Using the bathroom facilities on a plane is always an adventure in itself especially if it is your first time. Thank goodness, I had done this before. The room is so spacious that you can use the toilet, brush your teeth, wash your face, and blow your nose while not leaving the seat! I know that women are good at multi-tasking, but in here, we are amazing!

When I was finished and had started back to my seat, I noticed the breakfast cart was in the aisle next to the row just past our seats. I thought *oh no, I cannot get by it.* I was right. I sat or stood in the back of the plane until the flight attendant finished giving out the meals. When I got back to my seat, I saw that she had not left one for me, so I had to call her over. I asked her, “Are we ready to land yet?” By this time, I was hungry—until I got the meal, that is, and then I lost my appetite. Howard ate most of his. Men don't care as long as it's food.

After the plane landed, we went to retrieve our luggage. The handle was broken on my suitcase. I commented to my husband, “I don't know, Howard, we had a great vacation, but these airplanes are not being nice to me." We reported it, and the airline staff had a new one to give me right then and there. I asked Howard, "Do you think someone is missing new luggage?"

Howard said, "Quick, pick out a nice piece so we can go before the possible owner comes looking for it."

I giggled and grabbed a rather nice looking suitcase. Of course, I had to empty everything out of the damaged one, which is embarrassing because it was full of dirty laundry, but it all worked out and we were ready to call for a ride home.

"Let's go home," I said.

Howard said, "As soon as Rapid Rover gets here. The weather here is certainly not like Hawaii."

"At least it is not snowing or raining," I replied.

It seems like you go away for just a few days and there is the mail to look at when you arrive home, the phone messages, the laundry, the unpacking, and then there are all the stories about what happened to everyone, including the animals, while we were away. What got lost, who got hurt, who hit whom, and on and on it went. Then there was the jet lag to endure. Howard had some in Hawaii when we landed, but mine was saved for when I got home. For two days, I will be wide awake during the night and asleep at lunchtime during the day. But, as the saying goes, "there is no place like home".

The children were just getting up and eating breakfast as we pulled into the driveway early Thursday morning. You would have thought we had been gone for years. Of course, the happiest one was Margaret.

The children were yelling, "Mommy and Daddy are home!"

Our little informant was the first to greet us at the door. "Mommy, Daddy, we missed you. I gave Midnight a bath. Andrew got everything all wet, and Kit-Kat threw up a hairball," Susan said, speaking very fast.

"Wait a minute, *you* got everything wet and opened the door, and the wet dog got out and scared Mrs. Cooper," yelled Andrew.

Both Andrew and Susan said at the same time, "Kit-Kat fell into the bathtub and had bubbles all over!"

"Mom, I made lasagna for dinner, and it tasted really good," said Katie.

"Ah, home sweet home," I said as I gave them all hugs. "Well, I see you all survived! One by one you will have to tell your father and me all of the things that happened while we were away, and we can tell you about our trip, too."

"Yes, they all want to see their souvenirs," Margaret said, joining the welcome party at the door. "Did you both enjoy yourselves and have a good time?"

"Oh, it was just wonderful, Mom," I said. "Of course, the three flights over and back were not the best flights we have been on, but we did ok."

Howard was getting our luggage and paying the Rapid Rover driver.

"Hi, Son, how was it?"

"Oh, Mom, it was great. It was a shame I had to work those two days, but it gave Kim time to shop and rest by the pool."

"Look at your tans," Margaret said.

"I am jealous of your tans," said Katie. "Everyone here is white!"

"Really Mom, how is everything, and who scared Beverly?" I asked.

"When the kids washed the dog, she got out of the tub and ran through the house. Bev didn't expect to see a wet, large dog racing through the living room and family room. Her expression was priceless!" Margaret explained. "It was a Kodak moment, and I didn't have one."

"Is she going to come back?" I asked. "I bought a little gift for her."

"Oh yes, she came back on Tuesday. She is fine," said Margaret.

"Now where are the gifts?"

CHAPTER 3

Christmas is always a special time. The townspeople and the Skippack United Methodist Church together perform a live nativity on Christmas Eve. It is held in the park adjacent to the church after sundown. Mary, Joseph, the angel, the shepherds, the wise men, and a few live animals from a local farm come to worship the new baby, Christ the Lord. A baby doll is used for the baby Jesus. This live nativity goes on in all kinds of weather. It has only been cancelled twice for snowstorms. It is a privilege to be asked to be Mary or Joseph.

Tonight seemed peaceful and calm, which was unusual for us. Normally there is a lot of commotion with our four children. The beautiful autumn trees had shed their colorful leaves. The days were getting shorter. Tonight's sunset was magnificent. The glow of the sun sinking quietly behind the clouds gave the landscape a surreal quality. I could hear the wind whistling around the old windows as I pulled the curtains shut in our family room.

We moved to New England ten years ago. We were glad to get away from New Jersey's traffic and taxes. New Jersey is where Howard and I grew up, so it was our home, the place of our roots, but it was not where we wanted to raise our children.

We had vacationed in New England and loved the mountains and the scenic roads. The houses have a charm all their own. We love the quaint little towns, which typically consist of a library, a general store, and a grange hall. Taking a back road here can lead to adventure.

We almost settled in Vermont. One past December, Howard and I spent a weekend at the Trapp Family Lodge in Stowe. It was our mini vacation. We loved it. The Trapp Lodge is owned by the Von Trapp family made famous in the movie *The Sound of Music*. We certainly can understand why the Trapp family decided to settle here. The rolling hills make for a lovely setting. The lodge was decorated with garlands outside. Inside there were many real Christmas trees decorated with sparkling ornaments. Since my husband and I both love ornaments, we found it interesting and fun to admire the different trees. The dinner was elegant. We actually dressed up for dinner. Going out with four children, we never dress up. It snowed the entire time blanketing the hills to make the most beautiful picture. As we sipped our beverages in the lovely lounge, we listened to the piano music and sang some Christmas carols with the other guests.

We awoke to a beautiful morning with fresh snow covering the mountains. The breakfast buffet was delicious and abundant. We went cross-country skiing and took a sleigh ride. We ate lunch in their little luncheon room and browsed through the gift shop.

At first, the move to New Hampshire seemed difficult. Leaving our families, friends, jobs, and the only environment we had ever known was a big step in our lives. Howard had accepted a position as a chemical engineer for a large company outside Boston, Massachusetts, but we did not want to settle in Massachusetts. So, after checking out various schools, churches, and communities, we decided to settle in Skippack, New Hampshire. Of course, it is a bit of a drive for Howard to go to work, but he doesn't seem to mind. He was determined to live in either Vermont or New Hampshire. Massachusetts was just a bit too busy for us. Boston and the Cape have too much traffic.

It is so beautiful here in New Hampshire no matter what time of the year.

In the spring, everything is blooming, and the farm stands open for the season. It is like a breath of fresh air, especially if the winter has been very cold and the snow very deep. Everything awakens in this lovely time of the year. You can smell the fresh grass being cut and sometimes the not so fragrant smell of the fertilizer from the nearby farms. The hills are green and the cows are in the meadows. The many apple orchards are blossoming with fruit.

In the summer, there is so much to do. This is the best time to go into the White Mountains to Mount Washington. Then again, any time is a delightful time to go to New Hampshire's scenic White Mountains. Even in the summer, it can be very cold up there at 6,288 feet. We drove there once and were surprised to find that near the top of the mountain, the roads are just dirt. There is also a cog train that the children enjoy. Howard took the three older children last year to ride to the summit. I was nervous just watching them board the train. This train has the second steepest rack railway in the world. The average grade is over twenty-five per cent. The train moves slowly ascending the mountain at 2.8 miles per hour and descends the mountain at 4.6 miles per hour. They were on the train for sixty-five minutes going up and forty minutes coming down. For me it was too long of a ride. Susan said she was scared even though she sat with her daddy who had his arm around her for security. Of course, Katie and Andrew were brave and looking out over the mountain. Katie was snapping pictures. I believe Howard was bored. I could not wait until they returned down below.

The Kancamagus Highway, Route 112, is the scenic route and always fun; you might just see a moose. We saw one once on this highway when we first moved to New Hampshire. Actually, we were walking at dusk near the marsh. It was just Howard and I. It was a male moose and it was huge. Howard was so nervous and he fumbled with the camera; so our photos were not the best. The moose tours are interesting and fun. Everyone wants to see a moose. They are magnificent creatures; however, they are wild animals and can be very dangerous. The sad thing with all of our wildlife today is that we are taking away their habitats, and because of that, they are moving into ours. They can appear anywhere at any time. They blend so well into the environment that you do not see them until they are there, right in front of you. When you see their size, you wonder how you could miss not seeing them. They do not know to be cautious of cars or people. Unfortunately, many are involved in automobile accidents each year. When we see the *Brake for Moose* signs on the roads, we do just that. Some tourists want to run up to a moose and snap a photo, but that is not a smart thing to do. Moose have been known to charge at people and other animals if they feel provoked or threatened. A moose cow, a female, weighing perhaps eight hundred or more pounds and over six feet in height coming right at you can do a lot of damage. A male moose, or a bull, can stand over seven feet in height and weigh between eight hundred and fifteen hundred pounds! Ouch!

Along some roads are small waterfalls. People park their cars, get out, and just jump into the water. It is as refreshing as it is beautiful. Maybe I should rephrase that. The water is cold! There are many lakes in which to swim, fish, or go boating. Sometimes you can walk a trail or hike to a larger waterfall. We have done this a few times. Howard and I enjoy taking the children, Midnight, and a picnic lunch and spending the day hiking to the waterfall. We will tell the kids to put on their bathing suits and hiking shoes. I enjoy watching Susan as she picks up stones and inspects them before throwing them into the stream. Of course many times she likes the pretty stones and has to take them home where I will find them all over the house. She is the collector of things.

Autumn, of course, is spectacular with the fall foliage and many, many tourists. Lake Winnipesaukee is a wonderful vacation area for the family. You can rent a cabin or take a boat cruise on the lake. You can shop or hike. The scenery is just breathtaking. Lake Winnipesaukee sounds like the perfect vacation spot for next year.

Now it is winter—a wonderland of white. Usually, by late November or early December, we have snow, but this year the snow is late, and so far, the ground is not white. During the winter months the skiers, those riding in horse-drawn sleighs, and the snowmobilers love this snowy paradise. We truly hope we have snow soon for the skiing resorts and the children.

Here in New Hampshire, we have a fifth season. It is mud season. We have a mudroom. This is a room traditional to New England in which to leave one's muddy boots, wet gloves, and coats. It serves as a barrier between the indoors and outdoors. When the snow melts in early spring, the ground is wet with mud. Thank goodness for the mudroom. With a husband, two boys, two girls, a dog, and a cat, it is a welcomed addition to our house.

New Hampshire has a lot to offer. One special place is Annalee's Gift Shop in Meredith. The Annalee Company is celebrating their seventy-sixth year. Annalee was a lady who made dolls and sold them at local craft shows. She married a man named Thorndike. When there was no longer a profit from their chicken farming, she started her business of crafting dolls. Annalee's husband said that she had a vision, and that was, "If you smile, someone else has to smile back." Her dolls were all about the smile. Annalee passed away in 2002. Her dolls are still popular with collectors, and they sell in Christmas stores and gift shops across the country. There are dolls for every season of the year. I love the Christmas and Easter collections the best.

Besides the moose tours from spring through autumn, New Hampshire also has maple syrup tours, during which you can tap the trees for syrup. There are wonderful lakes for swimming or boating in New Hampshire. Portsmouth is on the ocean, and not far from there is the bridge to Maine. There you can go for the day and have lobster, visit a lighthouse or two, and shop at the outlets in Kittery.

New Hampshire also has no sales tax, which helps when shopping.

For the most part, Skippack seems to have remained unchanged throughout the years. It still has one main two-lane road with one lane heading north and the other heading south. The town is designed as a square with little lanes or streets bearing off from the center. Skippack reminds me so much of Bedford Falls from the wonderful Christmas movie classic, *It's a Wonderful Life*, one of my favorite movies. It is what I call a "feel good" movie, because when it ends you feel good that you watched it. Even though it is an old movie, our children need to watch these classic "good" movies.

Just think, every day our children watch us. They hear what we say and see what we do. When they are very little, they love to mimic what we are doing, and as they grow older, if anyone passes gas or burps, they giggle. To them it is funny and to us it is human, but embarrassing. They listen to everything except "clean your room and do your homework." Sometimes they may hear what we do not want them to hear. If someone says a bad word, a mental tape recorder starts running in their brain to record, remember, and repeat the bad word at a later time when you least expect it.

I remember older parents saying, "Do what I say and not what I do." That is not setting a good example. If you smoke cigarettes, your children will probably smoke or at least try it someday. It is the same way with drinking. If parents drink routinely during their children's upbringing, more than likely their children will drink when they are adults. Physical and verbal abuse at home is often reflected later in life. Abuse is wrong no matter who the victim is. We are supposed to live in a civilized world where there should be no abuse of any kind.

May the words of my mouth,
And the meditation of my heart
Be pleasing in your sight,
O Lord, my Rock and my Redeemer.
Psalm 19:14 (NIV)

Skippack is a charming town. It is more like a little village. People are friendly and say hi or good morning when they pass one another on the street. The amazing thing is that even though Skippack is a small town, the town shops prosper. Shopping is a pleasant experience because it gives us the chance to converse with our neighbors and friends and get to know the merchants.

Some of the shops and businesses are quaint, and many of them have unique names: The Market-Basket Supermarket; Luigi's Pizza and Italian Restaurant; Otto's German Bierhaus und Garten; the Lookin' Good Hair Salon; Fancy Fingers Nail Spa; the Candy Cupboard; Sweet Ums Ice Cream Shop; the Morning Brew Coffee House; the Pitter-Patter-Paw Pet Place (say that ten times fast); The European Baker; the Dew Drop Inn Bed and Breakfast; Crawford's Irish Pub; and Bauer's General Store. It almost sounds like a city more than a small town. Each shop has its own décor or specific architecture. The town is safe, and the residents can walk the streets without fear. So far, we have no McDonald's or fast food drive-through restaurants. The kids want that, and I am sure some day they will probably build here too.

During the winter months, the Sweet Ums Ice Cream Shop transforms into the Warm-Up Luncheonette. They have cold desserts during the summer and warm meals in the winter—smart thinking! Mr. and Mrs. Jenkins, the owners, are a wonderful older couple. They enjoy watching the little ones pick from fourteen delicious flavors of ice cream. Each one is familiar to the palate, but they give the flavors unusual names. I love the flavors of chocolate and peanut butter together. I was quite used to eating Moose Tracks ice cream, a delicious combination of chocolate, peanut butter, and fudge in vanilla ice cream. Here it is called Muddy Moose ice cream. Vanilla is White Nilla, Rocky Road is Bumps and Lumps, and Chocolate Chip Mint is Minty Chip.

I love their luncheon menu. The food is so good and homemade, and the price is right. Their homemade chili is out of this world. Mrs. Jenkins beats my cooking when it comes to navy bean soup. Mine is good, but Mrs. Jenkins's is excellent.

If you love animals, need to buy a gift, or have pets, a visit to the Pitter-Patter-Paw Pet Place is a must. It is decorated to look like a little dog or cathouse. They have just about everything you can think of to purchase for a pet. The prices are a little expensive, since many of the items are one-of-a-kind. The owners will special order items for their favorite pet customers. The children love to go in and browse, and they always want to buy something to bring home to our pets. I have seen everything from a barking photo frame to a frou-frou kitty bed and linens ensemble. You can purchase DVDs to play while you are at work so that your pets will not get lonely.

When you enter Bauer's General Store, a bell rings to announce your arrival. The building was formerly an old, large two-story house converted into a general store. Housewares, toys, and other items are displayed in bins or on tables and counters probably as they appeared a hundred years ago. Many items hang from hooks on the walls.

General stores are so much fun. They have everything from candy sticks to postcards to ointments for rough skin and dry heels. The children love to come here, but then again, so do I. Our whole family gets excited when we visit another town in Vermont, New Hampshire, or Maine that has a general store. There are many in the New England area, and each one offers many treasures to examine and buy. Locals in the surrounding area handcraft many of the items they carry. The children seem to get lost in the general stores, even in Bauer's. If you really looked at everything, it would take a very long time. There are so many things to interest children and adults. The bathroom facilities at Bauer's General Store are outside, one for men, and the other for women. They are designed to look just like outhouses used to, complete with a crescent moon on each door. When you open the door, the first thing you see is an old Sears catalog hanging from the wall for sentimental folks. Despite the fact that the outhouses look really old-fashioned, they do have flushing toilets, running water, and toilet tissue. Of course, in the winter they are heated somewhat, but going outside just to use the outhouse is a cold experience. Just think, in days of old, people used that Sears catalog instead of toilet tissue!

Mr. Bauer allowed our daughter Katie to help him in the general store last summer when she was only thirteen years old. It was her chance to earn a little spending money other than babysitting. The Bauers really love our daughter, Katie. She learned skills such as stocking the shelves and speaking with customers—friendly ones and the not so friendly ones. We have taught her to be polite to everyone. Mr. Bauer always says that the unfriendly ones must be from out of state!

The Bauers are wonderful people. They have lived here their entire married life. It seems they know just about everyone and everything in town. I would not call them gossiping people, as they are not vicious in any way; they are just well informed. In the store, they are a wealth of information and knowledge. If they do not know the answer to a question about something, they will find someone who does. They live by the values of being courteous and helpful. Two large plaques hang in the first room of the store. On one is written *I shall only pass this way once in my life, so let me do any and all the good I can.* As you leave the store, you see the other, which reads, *Do onto others as you would have them do unto you.* I say amen to both.

As you drive into town, you can see the Skippack United Methodist Church on the hill. The setting is so lovely that it was printed on postcards that sell in the general store. There is the Skippack Congregational Church of Christ and the Holy Child Roman Catholic Church at the other end of town.

Our little town even has the Elwood Covered Bridge. Tourists always stop to have their photograph taken either in front of or on the bridge, and they love the adjacent gift shop. The shop is adorable. The gifts are original to New England and to New Hampshire. There are little replicas of the covered bridge; items such as T-shirts, sweatshirts, and stuffed animals, including moose, bear, and deer; maple syrup products, Annalee dolls, and pottery.

I love the pottery. Most of it is a gray-blue color combination that can be personalized. As I mentioned earlier, I have collected many pieces as gifts from the children. One jar has our last name and one has our address. The pottery decorates our kitchen, which is also in the gray-blue color scheme. The pottery is made in New Hampshire. Many of the pieces feature blueberries. The shop sells something for every season of the year, and it is open year round. I truly love to shop here.

Of course, we have never stayed at the Dew Drop Inn Bed and Breakfast since we live here, but it is decorated so nicely like a little Victorian house. There are always flowers in decorative pots and dainty curtains at the windows. There is a large porch for when the weather is favorable. People can eat breakfast there or just sit and rock in the large rocking chairs.

CHAPTER 4

The schools are accredited in this county, and the people are friendly. Those are two things we definitely wanted in our new place to call home. Sometimes I feel like we are living in a storybook land or another country. Crime is low in our community and in the county. Of course, things do happen and the police are called, but thankfully nothing too terrible occurs. Usually it is quite peaceful here until it is harvest time in the fall or when the annual Christmas market occurs in December. Then it is anything but peaceful. The town comes alive.

The children love the harvest festival. There are hayrides, a scavenger hunt, a corn maze, and haunted trails at the many dairy farms on the outskirts of town. I lost Howard in the corn maze one year. The children made me find him! I sent someone in to find him, because I refused to go in there! He was teased for quite a long time about that. I believe that was the Christmas he received a New Hampshire map, a compass, and a whistle as gifts!

There are many fun things to do at the harvest festival. You can bob for apples, and there are contests for pumpkin carving, scarecrow making, pie baking, and for the best Halloween costume. The little ones particularly enjoy bobbing for apples and picking out pumpkins. The older children make the scarecrows and are very good at it when they are not arguing or fighting. Of course, I bake the pies. For this year I baked a molasses apple pie; now it's time to see if the judges will like it. The many pies are so delicious. These New Englanders really know how to bake. The cookies, cakes, and muffins made from pumpkin and apples are yummy. Their cooking is pretty good too. The soups are fantastic. One vendor makes huge salads.

"What a wonderful pumpkin you found, Kevin," I said to my little son as he sat in his stroller with a death grip on the little pumpkin he had picked from the pumpkin patch. To Howard, I said, "They will be judging the pies soon. I hope mine wins!"

"Mom, Dad, look at the scarecrow guy we made," said Andrew. "We did it together."

"Excuse me, if I had hearing aids, this would be the time to turn them up; what did you say?" I asked Andrew.

"Mommy, I tied the belt and helped to stuff him. See the straw?" Susan answered for her brother. She looked like she had been playing in a haystack. She had straw in her hair and all over her clothes.

"Yes, I see the straw."

"Dad, Mom, so what do you think? Can we put him out front for a decoration?" Katie asked.

"I am still trying to see the three of you working together on something and finishing it without fighting. I am in shock," I said.

"Yeah, but I sure like this scarecrow," commented Howard.

"Isn't he cool, Dad?" asked Andrew.

"Very cool," Howard said.

"We did it together, Mom," said Katie.

"I am looking for a place to sit down," I said.

"Susan stuffed it, Andrew picked out the shirt and pants, and I did the face," said Katie.

"Kathleen Suzanne, Andrew Mark, and Susan Mary, you all worked together to make a fine-looking scarecrow," I said. "Now are you going to tell me this was all a joke and you paid a lot of money to buy this scarecrow?" I asked.

"No, Kim, they really made it themselves; I was watching them," said Howard, and then he added, "Guess what our little boy did?"

"Pooped his pants, so now I have to change him?" I asked.

Howard laughed. "No, I don't think so; not yet. He rode on a pony."

"Oh, wow!" I said. "Did you enjoy your pony ride?" I asked Kevin. He just gave me a big smile in reply. "Did you take a picture of him on the pony?" I asked Howard.

"Yes, I did remember the camera," he said.

"Oh, I am proud of you for remembering," I teased.

"Kim, he was so funny. He was in awe of the pony. He stared at it and seemed timid, so I said, 'Giddy-up, giddy-up pony,' and he laughed so much." Changing the subject, he said, "How about we grab something to eat, and then we all head for home? Kevin is getting sleepy, and I am tired."

"Ok, but let me walk over to where the pie tasting is happening to see if the judges liked my pie," I said.

A short time later, Howard walked over and said, "So, did your pie win?"

"I got third prize," I said. "See, I have a yellow ribbon. Not too bad, and at least they liked it."

In the evening of the harvest festival, there is a bonfire and musical entertainment. Everyone joins in the singing. It is really a fun family event. By the time we return home, everyone is exhausted from being in the cool autumn air and enjoying the many activities.

December is my favorite time of the year. It is the annual *Christkindlmarkt*, the Christ Child market. It is held in the same location as the harvest festival. This is a German Christmas market patterned after the European markets. I love it. Many people living in this area are of German descent. A couple of neighbors on our street speak fluent Deutsche (German). We had traveled years before to the German Christmas Market in Mifflinburg, Pennsylvania, and enjoyed it so much that when we heard there was an annual one here, we were quite excited. This market is similar to the Mifflinburg market In Pennsylvania When you come to this market, you must dress very warmly and in layers, including a coat, gloves, a hat, warm socks, and shoes that cover your feet completely, such as boots. December in New England is cold, and the market is completely outdoors. The market goes on no matter what the weather unless there is a blizzard. The children's eyes light up when we tell them we are going to the Christkindlmarkt. We push Kevin in his stroller so if he gets tired he can fall asleep. He is plenty warm under all his covers. We allow Andrew and Katie to go ahead of us. They each have their cell phones so we can keep in touch. Andrew wants to watch the man on stilts. Susan is wearing everything but the rug in the car! She is bundled nice and warm. We are hoping for some snow flurries.

This market is open for three days in December. One street is closed to traffic, and the vendors have carts that look like small train cars or wagons lined along both sides of the street to sell their wares. As you enter the market, you walk under a welcome arch with two brightly lit trees on either side. These beautiful trees bear paper ornaments with the names of needy children or families in the area. When you take one of these names, it is suggested that you buy the present or grant the wish of the person on the paper. It gives you a good feeling to know that you are helping another child or family have a special Christmas. Sometimes it is a toy for a child or maybe it can be as simple as visiting a shut-in senior who has no family in the area. There is also a donation box, and each visitor is encouraged to contribute a dollar or more to help cover the cost of setting up the market.

As you walk through the market, you may see girl angels, the organ grinder with his pet monkey, or St. Nicholas himself. In the center of the cross streets is a large revolving pyramid with a nativity. On the last day of the market, there is a live nativity. On stage are German bands attired in their lederhosen and vests playing beautiful, traditional Christmas carols. The vendors offer so many wonderful treats, such as apple strudel, *Lebkuchen* cookies, *Spekulatius* cookies, hot chocolate, and mulled wine in a souvenir mug to keep. One vendor sells beautiful glass ornaments. The lights in the market are reflected in the ornaments making them twinkle and glow.

"Oh, Mommy, look at the beautiful ornaments. They sparkle like the stars in the sky," said Katie. "Look, there is the pickle like the one we look for on the tree every Christmas morning."

"Yes, the ornaments are all beautiful. They do twinkle and sparkle," I agreed with her.

"Andrew, I see you are eating already," I said.

"Yes, I am hungry and this apple strudel is so good," Andrew commented.

"Yes, it does look to be very good," as I watched him quickly devour the dessert.

"This year we are buying one of those prune men," said Howard. "I was telling a couple of the people at work about them and they seemed interested in seeing them. I hope they have some history information on them."

"That would be nice, Howard," I remarked. "Did you invite them to the market?"

"I mentioned it to them and I hung a flyer about it on the bulletin board. They seemed intrigued so maybe we might see them here," answered Howard.

German pickle ornaments hang in one corner. According to an old tradition, a pickle ornament is hidden on the tree, and the first child to find this ornament gets to open the first present. A beautiful hand-painted Christmas ball ornament is designed each year to commemorate the market, including the arch and the pyramid, and the market itself. There are jewelry vendors and handmade garments featuring sweaters and scarves. The homemade candy is scrumptious. One vendor sells wood-carved gifts from the Erzgebirge Mountains in the eastern part of Germany. These items are always beautiful and expensive. There are hand-carved trees, ornaments, music boxes, and more.

"There goes your mother into the shop with the expensive items. You kids be careful and do not break anything and be especially careful of the space heaters the vendors have in their little shops. We want nobody to get burnt," commented Howard. "Look, it is snow-flurrying," Howard said.

"Cool, Dad," smiled Andrew.

There is a chalet house for the children to play in at the market, and of course, the big man himself, Santa Claus, is there to hear their Christmas wishes.

"There's the Santa Claus house! See it," yelled Susan, and she was off running toward the chalet house.

It really adds a special touch if there is just a hint of snow in the air. Snowflakes are lovely as they land on our coats and hair as we walk through the market.

At the other end of the market are sleigh rides. Everyone sings Christmas carols as we ride along.

One vendor makes prune men. The prune men or *Zwetschgenmann* in German are a Nuremberg Christmas tradition. The vendor makes figures from dried fruits, including plums, nuts, raisins, figs, and prunes. Traditionally the prune men were made into chimney sweeps, but today they are made into many different figures. The prune figures are then displayed in the window facing to the outside so that no harm will come to those inside the house. In Germany, the tradition is if you see a real chimney sweep, you will have good luck all day. If you buy a little chimney sweep and display it in your home, you are supposed to have good luck as well.

As the nightfall descends, star-shaped lights draped on the outsides of each wagon light up and give the market a special glow. Then at six o'clock in the evening, the local schoolchildren hold their candlelit flashlights and walk through the market singing traditional German Christmas songs. Their voices are so pure and innocent as they sing the German versions of "O'Tannenbaum" ("Oh, Christmas Tree") and "Stille Nacht" ("Silent Night"). They invite everyone who knows these songs to join in the singing and be part of the parade. We learned the German version of Silent Night from our German neighbors. It is really worth standing in the cold and dark to see this parade of lights. This event is something we look forward to all year.

God blesses us with beautiful music and angelic singing.

When we arrived home, we all looked at the paper cutouts we had taken off the trees. Howard made a donation of ten dollars from our family to the market since he had not taken a name from the tree. Susan and Andrew both picked names of seniors in the local nursing home, who had written that they would like to have some children come and sing carols with them dressed in their Christmas clothes.

"Can we do it, Mommy?' Andrew and Katie asked.

"I certainly don't see why not," I answered. "Perhaps we can get some other children from school or the church to go with us. The more the merrier."

"What does yours say, Katie?" asked Andrew.

"An eight-year-old boy would like a special Lego toy set, and his six-year-old sister would like a doll," said Katie. "This is for two people instead of one."

"I think it is a good idea for me to have the paper ornaments now to see the names and where they live," I said. "This way, if you go to school with these children, no one will be embarrassed."

Their names are Arlene and Tyler, but I did not tell the children.

"Let me see the address," I said. "Oh, my, the address is the same as the one on my ornament. I believe it is on the other side of town near the railroad tracks. I do not think it is a nice area there. I do not mean a bad or scary area, but just not as nice as here where we live. We are blessed to live here, aren't we?"

"Mom, what was the wish on your paper?" Katie asked. "Is it another brother or sister?"

"No, this is the mother asking for groceries," I answered. "I will look into this tomorrow or the next day. I want to discuss this with your father, but maybe we can make this a very nice Christmas for them."

After the children went to bed, Howard and I discussed the requests. "It sounds like this family needs help," Howard commented.

"Yes, it sounds to me that the mother is fleeing from the husband and has the children, but no money to care for them. I do not see a phone number. The mother's name is Lenora Lee," I said.

"We will stop there tomorrow. Katie and Andrew can babysit for a little while," said Howard.

The next day we drove to the address on the ornaments. The apartment complex was very depressing to look at on the outside. Howard knocked on the door. A small-framed boy came to the front door.

"Hi, my name is Howard Turner and this is my wife, Kim," said Howard. The door opened wider and an attractive woman with a little red-haired girl stood in the doorway. "We would like to answer your requests from the Christmas trees at the Christmas market. May we come in?"

You could see the hesitation on her face, but then she opened the door wider and said, "Please, won't you both come on in? I am a bit embarrassed by the requests we put on those trees, but when I met Pastor Johnstone he was so nice. He said if I did that, then perhaps I could meet more people in town. He said the church folks would like to help my children, too."

I smiled. She had a lovely southern accent, and sounded like she was from Mississippi or Louisiana. She really was very pretty, thin, and petite. The children were well groomed too. The apartment was kept very nice.

"Please, sit down. I am just a little nervous about all of this; I hate to ask for charity," she said. "Oh, my goodness, my name is Lenora Lee and these are my children, Tyler and Arlene."

"Nice to meet you," we both said in unison. "We want to help you," Howard said. "Could we talk to you privately?" Howard asked.

"Of yes," Lenora Lee said, then to her children she directed, "You all go to your bedroom now."

"Lenora Lee, we know Pastor Johnstone and his wife personally because we go to that church," I said. "Where did you live before, and what brings you all the way up north to New Hampshire?

She giggled a little. "We are from Mississippi; Jackson, to be exact. My sister and her husband lived near here for a while and then moved back to Mississippi. However, her husband is accepting a job in Manchester, so they will be moving here the beginning of the year. Well, I mean they are moving between Christmas and the New Year holiday to be settled somewhere before he starts his new job in January."

"Are you planning to stay in our community?" I said.

"I would like to," said Lenora Lee. "I left my husband and want a divorce. He did not want to work, but he sure wanted me to work and do everything at home and with the children. Then he decided to take what money he made and drink all the time. When he came home drunk, he was not a nice man to be around, and he beat the children and me. He used to be a good husband and father, but he changed when he started going out and drinking. I called the police, but they did not do much. I took what money I could find in the house and in our bank accounts. I know that had to make him angry. Then again, in the beginning, I figured he would come looking for us, but I talked to my sister and she said he is already with a neighbor woman. We are just glad we got away. This town seems nice."

"May I ask your last name?" I asked.

"Oh yes, it is Jones; a real easy name to remember."

"Your children are in school here, right?" I asked.

"Yes, we have lived here for a couple of weeks," she answered. I did not know where to go or what to do in the beginning, so I stopped by the church and spoke with the pastor. He helped us get a place to live and food for a while. I looked for a job. I think I will have one soon in the general store. The Bauers are good folks."

"They are the best," we said. "What grade is your little girl in?" I asked. "Our daughter, Susan, is in the first grade. They may be in the same class."

"Yes, my daughter is in the first grade too. Miss Brooks is her teacher," she answered.

"Yes, they are in the same classroom. Tell me what toys they want exactly," I said. "Susan will not know. Can we keep this a secret from your children?"

"Yes, Tyler wants the Army Lego set. I was thinking that would be too expensive, though," she commented.

"They are not listening, I hope," I said.

"No, they are in their bedroom with the door shut. I hope to get a bigger apartment soon, because now they sleep in the same room," she said.

"Please don't tell them the toys are from us, because we want them to be friends with our children, and we don't want to embarrass anyone," I said. "You can tell them that Santa Claus brought the toys. What would Arlene like from Santa? Does she like playing with dolls," I asked.

"She wants the fancy Barbie doll; the Christmas Holiday Barbie," Lenora Lee said.

"Ok, no problem, and as far as dinner, you do cook here, right?" Howard asked her.

"Oh, of course, I do," she answered."

"You are not any different from us, Lenora Lee; you want the best for your children and for you, I said.

Lenora Lee laughed.

"You and I will go grocery shopping on Monday. Is that ok with you?" I asked.

"Oh yes, Monday will be fine."

"Ok then, I will pick you up on Monday at about ten o'clock in the morning. We will stop at the general store too. We are good friends with the Bauers. I think the church family will help you get on your feet."

"I don't know what to say," said Lenora Lee as tears welled up in her eyes.

"We're happy we've just made new friends," I said.

"Sometimes we all need a little help," said Howard. "This is not a handout; it is a hand-up."

On the way home, we stopped to see if Pastor Johnstone was home or at the church. Luckily, we found him at home.

We knocked on the door and his wife, Mildred, answered. "Hi there," she said, "Come on in and have a seat." Pastor Tom followed her and took a seat.

We explained to Tom that we had just met Lenora Lee and her two children, and that we were going to help them.

"Oh, you picked from the trees what the children want for Christmas," Tom said.

"Yes; we're going to buy the children some toys, and we'll buy some food so they can have a nice dinner," I said, and then I added, "I agreed to take her shopping on Monday."

"Tomorrow in church we are taking a love offering for them and that can be used for the food," Tom said.

"I would like to go shopping with you, Kim, if that is ok," Mildred said.

"Oh, of course you can," I answered. "We'll be going to Bauer's General Store; she said that he has offered her a job. I am sure they will need extra help with Christmas coming. Maybe we can do lunch at the Warm-Up Luncheonette."

"Sounds good to me," said Mildred. "I will look forward to it."

Tom explained what he and Mildred knew of Lenora Lee's story. "Yes, a couple weeks back Lenora Lee came to the church with her children and told us she had left her husband. She made her children wait outside in her car as she spoke with us. She said he was becoming violent and she feared for the children and herself. She has a good education and had a good job working at a bank for many years. She said she was very embarrassed going to work one day with a black eye. She still had some bruises when she arrived here in town. She said once he came home drunk and she was hoping to be in bed before he came in so there would be no confrontation. She was not quick enough. He started screaming and hitting and he physically pushed the children out of the bedroom, and then he pinned her to the bed and tried to choke her. She said he passed out and that is what saved her.

"She waited until he left the next day to get out of there while she and the children could. She took all the money she could get in a hurry and left while her husband was out. She had her sister keep watch so he would not come home and find them packing. The three of them hurried to pack their clothes and take what things they could throw in the car before he came home. Thankfully, she did have enough money for that apartment; she needs a bigger one, but that will have to do for now. I think with the help of the church members, and if she gets a job soon, she will be ok. Then she will have to deal with the husband and the divorce."

"I believe our church members will be generous this holiday," said Mildred.

CHAPTER 5

I heard Howard come in the back door. He remarked, "Boy, it is cold, and it feels like snow." He leaned over to kiss me, and I could feel the cold on his cheek. The weatherman has not predicted snow even though there is that chill in the air. It is common for snow to be on the ground for most of the winter here. So far this year we have had only a dusting but no real snow accumulation. Of course, the children want to see snow. They are all getting excited for Christmas and Santa Claus. The older two do not believe in Santa anymore, but I think everyone believes Christmas Eve. There is magic in the air, and no one wants to take a chance on not believing. Susan is the most excited. She is now in first grade and the class is rehearsing songs for the school program. She is ecstatic that she is going to sing "All I Want for Christmas Is My Two Front Teeth." She is missing one tooth in the front, and by Christmas she may be missing both of her front teeth as the other one is loose. The song is perfect for her.

Thank you, God, for eyes to see, ears to hear, and a voice to sing.

Howard said he was letting the dog out for the last time tonight. Then I gave both the cat and the dog their treats. Midnight, our three-year-old female Labrador, is so good with the children. Actually, she acts like one of the children. We adopted her from a local animal shelter. Andrew fell in love with her immediately. She loves to play in the snow, and in the summer, she is the fifth kid in the pool. She will circle the pool deck barking loudly before jumping into the pool. If they are playing a game with a ball, she wants the ball. Andrew always denies that she sleeps on his bed, which is so funny, because he is asleep and there she is asleep next to him on the covers. She is the most protective of him out of all the children. He was almost eight when we adopted Midnight as a puppy. He walked Midnight and taught her to say please, give her paw, and play dead.

Kit-Kat, our cat, was a stray. The veterinarian figures Kit-Kat is about two years old. He loves to cuddle and purr. He is a calico with white feet. He loves it when Andrew sets up the racecars. He waits for the cars to be in place on the racetrack. He quietly watches until they come within reach. Pounce! He either knocks the cars off the track or chases them when they move. It is fun to watch him play. Of course, when I clean I find little cars under the furniture. He is the funniest cat I have ever seen. He is always looking for trouble. When it is cold outside, both animals love to lie in front of the fireplace to get warm, but then again, so do I. The cat mostly with Katie. She is the true cat lover in our family.

ourse, we are all animal lovers and believe that eak up for them and protect them. We need me, and larger fines for people who do not take care of their animals. There should be no animal abuse, or even worse, child abuse. Usually, people start harming animals, and then they go on to harm small children; anything or anyone that is smaller or defenseless. We must protect our wildlife, sea life, pets, and children. Pets cannot take care of themselves, so it is our responsibility to do so, and to report to the authorities those who do not.

We do see more wildlife here than we did in New Jersey—besides the children, I mean. The children are always hoping to see a big moose with a large rack of antlers, or a mother moose with her young ones. They are so cute to watch. There are more moose sightings farther north. Occasionally, people see moose, deer, or bear here in Skippack. I can wait to see a bear, but I love to see deer. We see more deer here than moose. Our friend had a moose in her yard. She thought at first it was a horse, and she went to get her camera. When she went to snap the photo, she realized it was a female moose.

Our friends have seen bear tracks in their yard. One night while they were sleeping, they were awakened by a loud bang. They thought someone was trying to break into their house. When they went downstairs, they could see on their outside deck that two bear cubs had climbed the birdfeeder and broken it, causing them to fall onto the deck. When our friends saw the mother bear, they quickly retreated. If you see bear cubs, more than likely the mother is nearby. A mother bear will attack to protect her cubs. They are wonderful animals, but they are not the cuddly little stuffed bear toys children play with. We keep all our trash and recyclables in the garage so as not to attract any bears or other animals. Raccoons will take the lids off the trashcans and spill trash everywhere.

We were told there are cougars in this area, but fortunately, we have never seen them. It does not hurt my feelings that we have never seen them. Sometimes we see fox and fisher cats. I never knew what a fisher cat was until we moved here. The fisher cat is not a feline, but is a North American marten related to the weasel family. It can climb trees easily. The fisher cat kills porcupines. I find them quite ugly, and they screech in the night and sound almost like a child screaming. It is a scary sound to me, and one I do not care to hear. They are certainly not my kind of animal.

CHAPTER 6

If houses could talk, I think many of the houses here would have a story to tell. Many are quite old. Most are large with several adjoining rooms. They have character that seems to favor the elegance of the past. Many houses have connecting porches or breezeways, garages, and then a barn similar to many of the houses with attached barns in Europe.

Other houses have that Victorian style or gingerbread effect. Since I am a *Jersey girl*, these houses remind me of Cape May, New Jersey. Cape May is famous for its gingerbread eyelet trim on the houses. These houses are said to have eyebrows because of the trim. The houses have peaks, gables, and porches. Some have what are called widow's walks. A widow's walk was also called a widow's watch. It is a railed platform on the rooftop with a small, enclosed cupola. Many nineteenth century North American houses in New England have a widow's walk. They provided a way for the wives of mariners to watch for when their husbands returned from being at sea, but many times the ocean had taken their lives, leaving the women widows.

Our house is a two story with a small third-floor attic. It is the typical New England style with an open wraparound porch and railing. In the nice weather, we have wicker furniture on the porch. Our windows are very tall, and are framed by wooden shutters. The front door has etched-glass panels on either side of it. We have a family room with a fireplace, a living room with a bay window, which has a stained glass panel in the center, and a long dining room. These rooms are unique. There are little windows with window seats where I place house plants and sometimes sit to read if I can without being reported missing. There are shelves and doors that open small closets for storage. When we first moved in, Katie and Andrew would play hide and seek in these small closets.

All the rooms have doors, such as the French doors between the living room and dining room. The doors keep the lived-in rooms a bit warmer when the power is out due to a storm. We can close off that room while keeping another room warm with the generator we purchased a few years back. We found out it is no fun being without heat, electricity, or water for a few days. That happened once, and once was enough to prompt us to buy a generator. The house was too cold and dark. Firewood is stacked in piles by the shed for the fireplace, which also helps keep us warm out of necessity when there's no power, or just for the enjoyment of it.

We have an eat-in kitchen that we remodeled shortly after moving into the house. Now we have marble counter tops, lovely oak cabinets, and a flat range oven. There is a breakfast nook off the main kitchen. I love it. It is bright and cozy.

We have upstairs and downstairs bathrooms, three bedrooms, three walk-in closets, a basement, a mudroom, a laundry room, and the attic. There is a small-enclosed porch on the second level that we will eventually turn into a bedroom for Kevin. Since Andrew is already eleven, he does not want a little brother sharing a room with him much longer. The age difference is just too much. At the present, he does not mind, because Kevin is still in a crib. Soon, very soon, he will be walking. I can hear Andrew complaining already.

The children play darts and pool in the basement. Thank goodness, it is a deep basement so we have plenty of headroom to walk around. Howard has an office down there. My office consists of a secretary desk in our bedroom. Of course, I really do not need an office, but Howard does for his job. He has a television and a recliner too in case he just wants to get away and rest for a little while. He sometimes falls asleep down there. When I go down to the pantry to get something for the kitchen, he wakes and looks at me ruefully, and he usually says, "I know I should be at the gym or exercising right here on the stationary bike, but this recliner feels mighty comfortable right now."

I said, "Well, when you go to the doctor for your next check-up, he will tell you that the handle of your recliner does not qualify as an exercise machine!"

Katie is still complaining she has to share her room with her six-year-old sister even though she is now fourteen years old and a teenager. She hates it. However, for now they share a room, just because we are such *awful* parents. Our answer to her is, "Get over it." When they are angry with each other, they string a clothesline across the room and drape sheets over it to separate each side. All we hear then is "Don't come on my side of the room!" or "Mom, she is on my side and touching my stuff." Then there is the cell phone dilemma: "Mom, she is listening to my conversation." Ah, sisterly love. Praise the Lord; they really do love each other. Maybe if we do not go crazy, they will stop arguing by the time they are out of high school. By then it will be war between Andrew and Kevin.

Of course, Katie has her things just the way she wants them. She is the neat one. She has her posters of the Jonas Brothers and Justin Bieber and stuffed animals just a certain way, and of course, a little sister touching them is off limits. Her clothes are always picked up and put away.

Susan loves her American Girl dolls and Barbie dolls, but she is not as neat. I find things under the bed and on the floor on her side of the room. Sometimes clothes are hanging out of the drawers. Both girls seem to like books, which make us happy. Katie is an avid reader.

I do love this big, old house even though it is a lot of maintenance both inside and out. I know that inside these walls love and happiness exists.

Thank you Lord for food to eat, an inviting welcome to all who enter, and a place to call home.

It is not easy to maintain a healthy weight with a big family to feed. I try to cook healthy meals for all of us. Thank goodness for one-pot meals. They are usually very filling for the stomach and are easy to prepare. I try to make sure the children eat the foods they should and not junk food. I want them to keep a sensible weight. I make sure they get outside and get some fresh air and sunshine too. So many of the children today are glued to the computer and do not get any fresh air or sunshine.

Tonight's dinner is pork and sauerkraut. I cook it the way my mother taught me. I put the pork and sauerkraut in a large pot and let it cook until it falls apart. Then I make dumplings for the top. Of course, we must have creamy mashed potatoes, too. We all take turns saying grace, and this evening was Susan's turn. I gave her my Mom look that implies I want her to say it correctly and not silly. She sweetly said, "God is good, God is great, let us thank him for our food. Amen." She wanted to say, "Grace in the kitchen, Grace in the hall, good God, Grace, don't eat it all." This was a little something she brought home from first grade.

The children were done with their homework—or that is what they told me. Actually, they all do well in school; their report cards are filled with As, Bs, and an occasional C. After dinner they could watch television or play with the new Wii computer game. We try to encourage them to play games or read.

It has been a week since the Christmas market. December is a busy month. Today is a miserable rainy day. I pour myself a cup of coffee and sit in the breakfast nook. Here come the "little kids"—the dog and cat. They are looking for their morning breakfast. I let Howard sleep later this morning. This is great. The children are still asleep, it is Saturday, and I have a few quiet minutes to myself.

Suddenly, I hear footsteps. Well, so much for my few quiet minutes.

"Mom," said Andrew, "This is the first Saturday of the month. We want to have our pictures taken with the Clydesdales before Christmas."

"That's right, I almost forgot. I am glad you remembered. I guess I forgot to put it on the calendar. Let your dad sleep a little longer and then you can wake him so we can make plans," I said. My calendar is like my Bible. I write everything on it that is happening for that day, and I keep track of everyone's birthday and age. I have a very large calendar! It is on the side of the refrigerator. I do not know if the refrigerator holds up the calendar or the calendar holds up the fridge. There are so many notes clipped to the calendar. "I must put up a clipboard sometime soon," I murmur to myself.

A few minutes later, Howard walked into the kitchen carrying Kevin. "There are my two sleepy heads," I say as I kiss him and the baby good morning. "Howard, we almost forgot about taking the children to have their photos taken with the Clydesdale horses. We could make it a fun afternoon. The kids will want to visit the gift shop, and then we could stop at the Bierhaus for an early dinner. I will call and see if we need reservations for both the pictures and the dinner."

"Yeah, I forgot too. I hope it stops raining before we leave," said Howard. "It seems windy too. It is just a miserable day. Hey, how about I make breakfast for all of us this morning?" he said.

"That would be nice, thank you. I will set the table and call the other kids to get up," I said. "I can help by getting some of the ingredients out for you. What do you plan on making this morning?"

"How about I make pancakes with sausage and bacon. Do we still have some fruit salad from yesterday?" asked Howard.

"Yes, we have enough for breakfast," I said. I took the baby and Howard set about making breakfast. One by one the other two woke up. I put Kevin in his highchair and set the table.

"Mom, Dad said breakfast is ready," yelled Susan.

I walked into the kitchen. "Susan said that breakfast was ready, but I didn't hear the smoke alarm go off," I said.

Howard gave me a silly grin and said, "That is when you cook bacon!"

"Daddy made breakfast this morning."

In unison it was, "Thank you, Daddy."

The Anheuser-Busch Brewery is located in the town of Merrimack, which is only about an hour's drive from our house. This is home to the world-renowned Clydesdale horses. It is called the Clydesdale Hamlet. On the first Saturday of each month from 1:00 p.m. until 3:00 p.m., you can pose for a picture with one of the Clydesdale horses. The Hamlet is decorated quite lovely for the holidays. I made sure we arrived early because it was the first weekend in December and I knew it would be crowded. The Clydesdales are magnificent horses. They are beautiful in the way they strut along pulling the Budweiser wagon. Their huge white hoofs stand out as they clump along the road. After our mother passed, my sister and I took our father on a weekend vacation to Williamsburg, Virginia, and we went to see the Clydesdales at Busch Gardens. There is so much to see there. Of course, we did not do any of the rides, but we really enjoyed the many shows. We also went to Historic Colonial Williamsburg. My father really enjoyed himself. Of course, Dad has visited the Clydesdale hamlet here on many trips, too. He really loves the horses.

I think of the television commercials featuring these talented horses. I think everyone remembers the television commercial in which the horses knelt down in a solemn bow overlooking New York City. It was beautiful and touched many hearts. This commercial aired only one time so that no profits would come of it. The commercial was in memory of the tragic event that occurred on September 11, 2001.

We must never forget.

Katie felt she was too old for pictures with the horses and expressed her feelings by mumbling little comments and making faces. "You better stop it, Katie," I said. "You better smile and not ruin this for your brothers and sister. If you do not want to come after this year that will be fine, but please just try to enjoy it this one last time."

"Oh, Mom, I just am not into this stupid photo anymore."

"Well, you better get into it now. You are next having your photo taken; smile!"

The photos did turn out nice. The photographer had Kevin giggling and took the photo at the perfect moment. Everyone in line behind us was laughing at little Kevin. He looked so cute in his Santa outfit with the hat to match. The words on the hat read, *Santa, could you define naughty?* Susan wore a corduroy jumper with a Christmas blouse. She was so adorable; she looked like a little elf. She asked if she could wear her little tiara. This is a fun photo so I told her yes. Now she looked like a little princess. Andrew wore his soccer shirt with reindeer antlers; perfect for his photo. Katie wore a sweater with snowflakes. She looked lovely yet casual.

"The horse looks great in this picture," Howard commented to Andrew.

Andrew answered, "Better than my two sisters look!"

"Kevin is the cute one—you are ugly!" shouted Susan.

"Yeah, you are the dumb-looking one," teased Katie. "Stop touching me!"

"You're stupid!"

"No, you're stupid."

"You won't get anything for Christmas."

"Yes, I will; Santa likes me."

"Ok, that's enough," snapped Howard. "Let's not ruin the day. It is miserable driving in this rain, and we are going to the German restaurant for dinner, so stop with the name calling."

The restaurant was beautifully decorated for Christmas. There was a real tree with German ornaments, and decorative items such as cuckoo clocks, animals, the German pickle, beer barrels, and more. Sparkling garland was draped on the tree branches. A beautiful angel with feathery wings stood at the top of the tree. Poinsettia garlands hung around the room. There was a large, real wood-burning fireplace and we could see someone tending to the fire.

This restaurant is always a happy place at any time of the year. From the end of September through the beginning of October is the Octoberfest celebration. They have vendors selling German candy and pastry. Some vendors sell German jewelry and clothing. They usually have entertainment from Germany, too.

"Look, Mommy, they have a pretty angel on top of the tree," Susan said as she pointed to the treetop.

"Oh yes, she is quite lovely," I said.

Dinner was delicious. We ate veal cutlet (*Wiener Schnitzel*), noodles (*Spatzle*) gravy, applesauce, vegetables, rolls, and a raspberry torte for dessert. The German music was festive. Some customers were dancing and some were singing with the band. The waitresses were dressed in their traditional dirndls. A dirndl is a jumper with a lacy or low-cut blouse. The dirndl may lace up in the front, too. Sometimes they wear an apron. Our waitress loved making Kevin smile. He was having a happy evening until he began to get sleepy. It was then time to leave. He was cranky and tired. We left and spent the rest of the evening at home watching television and relaxing, something we seldom have time to do. Even the cat and dog seemed to want to cuddle tonight. I think being out in this wet, chilly day has made everyone want to snuggle and get warm.

"We should get a tree soon. How about tree hunting this Friday night?" asked Howard. "The Boy Scouts will be selling trees again this year. Do you remember that beautiful Douglas fir we bought last year?"

"Yes, but I mainly remember that we had to cut down that very large, beautiful Douglas fir tree," I commented. "Yes, this year is Andrew's turn to cut down our Christmas tree. Is that ok with you, Howard?"

"Sure, but if he needs help, we will all be there to pitch in. Most of the outside decorating is done," Howard commented.

"Hey, Dad, bet I can beat you at darts," said Andrew.

"Oh, I don't think so," yelled Howard as they both ran down the basement steps to play a game.

The outside lights did look nice. With Katie's help, Howard had draped the lights along the edges of the house, on the shrubbery, and in the trees. The gazebo in the side yard had lights and a Santa and reindeer. I have an electric lighted candle in each window of the house, and I made the wreath for the front door.

I love to do crafts. The challenge is finding the time to do them. Katie and I like to make things together. At only fourteen, she is talented, artistic, and has a real flare for styles and colors. During the year, we make seasonal wreaths to sell at the church bazaar in December. We usually work on these downstairs in the basement during the winter months when it is too cold to go outside. Having our workspace in the basement helps us to be productive because we can make a mess and leave it to clean or put away later.

Our house is big, but something mysterious happens when we buy a tree and bring it home. All the rooms seem to shrink in depth and width. I always laugh as Howard has to literally push the tree through the door and drag it across the room only, to acknowledge that it is too tall. Sadly then he must cut off the top. The tree is always beautiful once we decorate it with lights, reflectors, ornaments, and tinsel.

I mentioned to Howard, "I think next year we should invest in an artificial tree with the lights already on. There are so many beautiful ones—and no more tinsel! It would be easier and quicker to decorate, and besides, our lights are really getting old, and I think after this year we should get rid of them. I do not feel safe using them when they are so old. And I can do without tinsel." I would never put tinsel on an artificial tree because you cannot take it off easily and it would look bad for the next year.

When decorating the Christmas tree, we use the old, big lights with the aluminum reflectors. They belonged to my parents. These lights bring back memories of my father complaining that my mother had too many Christmas decorations. She would ask my sister and me to untangle the strands of lights so she could put on the reflectors and screw in the light bulbs. Of course, we had to make sure no two colors were next to each other.

"Kim, we can always just buy the strings of lights with the larger bulbs so that they look old-fashioned," said Howard.

"We will have to think about it."

Howard, the children, and I decorate the tree together, but only Andrew, Katie, Howard, and I put on the tinsel. As much as I hate tinsel, I must admit that a real tree always looks dressed with tinsel. The kids, however, get to fighting over how to put it on, and the silver strands end up everywhere, but not on the tree. What a mess! We do not want the animals to eat the tinsel. It could be deadly for them. The cat and dog do not get into the tree, so we are lucky in that regard.

The children all get to put on their own ornaments. Howard and I started a Christmas tradition with the birth of each child. Every Christmas, until the children leave home to be on their own, we buy them a special ornament. In the beginning, we bought them a chest to store the ornaments properly so they would not get broken. Each year they can pick out the ornament of their choice. It can be anything they like. Then when they marry, this same box of ornaments will decorate their first Christmas tree together. It is their heirloom.

Ornaments are wonderful. Ornaments can tell a lot about a person and his or her life. When we show our tree to visitors, we tell them, "Oh yes, there is a tree under all those lights, ornaments, and tinsel!" Whenever we travel, I always look for Christmas shops. Years back, we went to one in St. Petersburg Beach, Florida. The shop was decorated beautifully and had many different items compared to what we normally see in New England. Of course, with the shop being in Florida, many decorations have to do with the beach and seashells.

Howard always says, "A Christmas shop! I will take the baby and the younger two for a walk while you and Katie shop. No way do I need to be responsible for little children in a shop with so many beautiful, expensive, breakable ornaments and collectibles."

The children's Santa wish lists were written in advance—way in advance. Did they start last January? I believe they keep adding to them. We still had to plan a family shopping day at the mall. I usually take the girls and Howard takes the boys. At school, the little ones have a Santa shop and of course, the most precious gifts are bought there. Gifts are donated to the Santa shop, or the PTA buys little items for the children to purchase for their parents and other relatives.

This year we planned to get skis for Andrew. Of course, that means all of the other stuff too, like poles, ski pants and a jacket, a hat, gloves, socks, ski boots, and even ski lift tickets. He seemed interested when we spoke about it earlier in the year, so that's what we're getting him. Since Susan is still so little, we will get her ski lift tickets, an outfit, and rent the other items. There's no sense spending a fortune if she lacks interest in skiing. We may give her ice skates, too. Katie knows how to ski and ice skate, but she does not seem to have the time or the transportation. Howard and I used to ski and skate, but we have not done so in years. I am sure we will try again this year with Andrew. Well, maybe just Howard will!

My dream was always to be a figure skater. I love to watch the young ladies move across the ice. They are so graceful and so young. I am in awe of the couples who do the ice dancing. They are so coordinated, and all their moves are precisely in time with each other. They certainly make it look easy. When the fellow lifts the girl, I pray he does not drop her. Instead, they just glide along the ice in perfect harmony. Katie belongs to the Appalachian Mountain Club. It is a supervised club for teens. The mission of this club is to educate teens to become leaders. They promote protection, enjoyment, and understanding of the mountains, forests, waters, and trails. The land area involved with the Appalachian Trail is from Maine to Washington, DC. They camp, hike, cross-country ski, and more. She enjoys it, and the adults seem passionate in teaching the teenagers.

Ah, Christmas, the most wonderful time of the year. It is busy, hectic, and unfortunately always expensive, but I love it. I am always puzzled in the grocery stores. They are stocked with all the baking items, the trimmings, and all the different candies and cookies that you never see any other time of the year In the men's haberdashery department, you will find stocking stuffers such as desk calendars, remote control caddies, monogrammed handkerchiefs, and miniature dart boards. Just try to go into the same department in July and ask for men's handkerchiefs or miniature dartboards. First, the sales person will look at you as if you have two heads. They have not a clue as to what they look like, much less, where they are.

I have never figured out nor should I say I am amazed that in our country we do not have a St. Nicholas or Santa Claus Day! Many other countries have a Santa Claus Day and Christmas Day. Germany's St. Nicholas Day is December 6, which is when Santa Claus brings the toys to the children. They also give gifts on Christmas Eve when they celebrate the holiday with their families.

We commemorate so many other special days, such as Administrative Professionals Day, Grandparents' Day, Groundhog Day, Valentine's Day, St. Patrick's Day, Boss's Day, to name a few, so why don't we have a St. Nicholas Day or Santa Claus Day and leave Christmas to be what it should be—a day to celebrate the birth of Jesus, the Savior, Christ the Lord and King of Kings? I think to myself, *who do I write to about this? Do I write to the president or a senator? Who?* I really do not think I am crazy for feeling this way. It does surprise me, though, that no one else has ever tried to institute a Santa Claus Day. So many people get caught up in the holiday shopping, parties, decorating, and entertaining that they forget what the holiday is all about. When I see cards with the words Merry Xmas on them, I could scream. I know the Xmas is acceptable, but

I do not approve of it. I tell the children we must always keep *Christ* in Christmas. He is what Christmas is all about. Xmas is not a holiday at our house.

Christ is Christmas.

CHAPTER 7

Since Friday night was so cold, we waited until Saturday morning to go tree hunting. Luckily, it did not take long for us to pick out a tree.

I spoke my famous last words again this year. "I think it is too big."

"Nah," said Howard. "We need a large tree because we have so much to put on it. Where's Susan?"

"You can't see her; she is behind the tree!" I said, but it didn't seem to matter what I said.

It looked huge, but Howard said it would look *grand* in the family room. Grand? Is that another word for too big? The children may have visions of sugarplums dancing in their heads, but I have visions of tree sap, pine needles, and tinsel on the rug. Susan asked if she could help Andrew cut down the tree. Howard told her that she must ask her brother since it was his turn. Reluctantly but kindly, Andrew said yes. Of course, Daddy and the salesman did the actual cutting of the tree. The Boy Scouts received a percentage of the sale.

After taking the tree home, we left it in the garage and decided to go to the mall. We must be crazy to go on a weekend, but we do not have that many weekends left before the holiday, and this time seemed to work best for everyone. This will be our last time for mall shopping before Christmas. Katie will go with her friends. Finding a parking spot at the mall is always challenging. Patience is a must!

"A plane could land easier than us finding a place to park," Howard said. "Do they have a shuttle bus?"

"No, dear, I do not think so, but it is a good idea," I answered. "I guess this is why online shopping has become so popular."

"Now remember to keep your cell phone on so we can catch up with each other when it is time to go home," said Howard.

"You know my cell phone is on," I said. "If by some miracle we see a parking place, maybe I should get out and stand in it until you can pull into it."

"I don't know if that is a good idea. With the way cars are buzzing around in this parking lot you either would be run down or packaged and thrown in the trunk with the rest of the presents," Howard said.

"Oh there, Howard, quick, let me out before the confused man in that car pulls into our parking spot!" I shouted.

I jumped out of the car when it was safe to do so—that is, if anything is safe in this parking lot. I walked over to that parking space and stood in it. Well, if the man wasn't confused before, he was now.

He pulled near me and looked at me. I motioned and told him my husband was pulling into this spot. I said Merry Christmas to him, but I do not think he could hear me with the window closed. It was difficult for me to read his lips! It didn't look like he said Merry Christmas to me. I called out, "Are you going to eat with that mouth?" I am sure he did not hear me.

"What are you doing?" Howard asked. "He was angry we took this spot, and no, he probably did not say Merry Christmas. Kim, you have to be careful; people are crazy out here, and have you ever heard of road rage? It is like the Indy 500 here. By the way, that man didn't appear to be smiling as he pulled away."

"I was polite," I said. "He just didn't like me standing in the parking spot he wanted."

"You are amazing, Kim," Howard said, and he kissed me. "Thank you; if you hadn't done that, we would still be riding around looking for a space."

Katie had agreed to stay home and babysit Kevin. Bless her. Besides, she is a teenager and does not want to be seen shopping with her family. Naturally, she wants to shop with her girlfriends. Her friend's mother will take them to the mall, and that way they can eat lunch in the food court, buy their gifts, check out the teenage boys, and actually look for things they will want to buy after Christmas when everything is on sale and it is time to exchange everything.

I set off with Susan in tow, and Howard went in another direction with Andrew.

The mall decorations were so lovely. Garlands with huge balls and sparkling lights were placed across the main entrances. Holiday lights make everything look festive. At nighttime, the lights shine like stars in the sky. Santa Claus was in the grand court greeting children. That area was very crowded. There was a Santa Claus train running from one end of the mall to the other for the children to ride. Animated animals were moving back and forth. Santa's elves were escorting the children to Santa or the train. The kids looked so cute in their Christmas clothes to have their photo taken with Santa. Some families dressed alike to have their photos taken. One family was wearing red and green, and another family had chosen to wear funny pajamas. The father had the flap with snaps in the back. There were many kiosks in the center of the mall with vendors selling special Christmas items such as handmade ornaments, sports paraphilia, Christmas stockings, dog and cat items, and calendars, just to name a few. We only buy certain things here because we know we can buy things locally in town. Most of the shops in town offer beautiful gift-wrapping or printed boxes and bags. Each child has his or her own allowance money to spend on presents.

"Remember, Susan, we will see Santa at another time in the general store when it is not so crowded. We will take you and Kevin. We won't forget."

"Ok, Mommy," she said, but I knew in my heart she really wanted to tell him right here and now what she wanted for Christmas.

While walking past the fragrances in a department store, a woman who apparently just had a facial was handing out little fragrance tabs as samples to entice customers to buy. Of course, you can bet your buttons she has that bottle of perfume in her other hand ready to spray you with the fragrance at any given second. Her finger is already on the trigger. I say, "No, thanks, I am allergic," only because after two or three shots of these perfume spritzes, I will have one bad headache by the time I get back to the car. Either that or I will spend half the day in the ladies' room trying to wash off all those "heavenly" scents. If I don't wash them off, the blended smell of them is something like a strong industrial cleaner. And---that pretty bottle of cologne only costs about eighty dollars!

Holiday music was playing in the mall. I enjoy hearing that. I guess it is because I am older, but it really bothers me to go into a nice department store and try on an expensive dress only to have to listen to loud rap music. I do not want to hear that. If the store feels compelled to play some kind of music, it should be seasonal or easy listening music. Rap music makes you nervous, but easy listening music is just that—it is easy to listen to because it is more relaxing. Save the rap for the kids.

As we strolled through the mall, I watched my young daughter. Susan looked so cute walking in her patent leather shoes and her dress coat. Her shoes clicked as she walked along. She was swinging her little matching shoulder bag. I thought to myself, *she is very fashionable.* She looks like a grown-up girl even though she is only six years old. She talked the entire time. It was funny listening to her. You could hear the excitement in her voice and the anticipation of the holiday in her eyes.

"Mommy, here is the toy store where we can look for Kevin's present. Oh, look Mommy; I want to tell Santa I want that doll," Susan commented looking in the store window. "Oh, I am going to ask him for that game, too"

"I know you would love to look or play with everything and I feel badly that we cannot do that today, but we are here to shop for gifts," I said. "I am sorry. Maybe after Christmas, I mean in January, we can come for the day and just look and play with some of these things and have lunch here. Does that sound like a plan?"

"Yes, Mommy, it sounds like a good plan to me," smiled Susan. I had to chuckle to myself she spoke so sweetly.

Susan wanted a stuffed animal for Kevin. I dreaded going into the toy store because it was so crowded, and I knew I would never get my little girl out of here once we went in. Despite my hesitation, we went into the store. A giraffe was Susan's choice for Kevin. I liked it too. Of course, it was difficult, to say the least, to get her out of the toy store. She saw things she had asked Santa to bring to her for Christmas. She said it was a secret what she was buying for her daddy and me, and that those presents were at school. She would buy them at the Christmas store. She wanted hair clips for Katie. She had seen her older sister looking in *Girl's Life* magazine commenting that she liked them. Now, what to get for Andrew? He really likes the show *Family Guy*. Susan found a T-shirt showing *Family Guy* characters and thought Andrew would like it. I said ok. Some of the T-shirts are not acceptable to me.

Susan and Andrew are still so excited about Christmas. Katie is older now, and sure, she is happy about Christmas and what it means, but that childlike excitement is gone. Some parents believe that we should not tell our children there is a Santa Claus because it is a fantasy, but the magic that comes with the fantasy is wonderful for children. They are only little once. The books and movies are mostly fantasy, too, and we do not take those away from them, so we should let them pretend that Santa Claus is real for a brief few years in their lives. It encourages them to use their imaginations to be creative.

Howard and Andrew enjoyed spending the afternoon together. Andrew wanted to buy a long sweater with a tie belt around the waist for Katie. He picked the color pink.

"Your sister will look nice in that," commented Howard. "The sweater is soft and so is the color."

For baby Kevin, Andrew wanted to purchase footed pajamas. "Dad, when I go in to see Kevin, he is never under his covers, so this way his feet will stay warm. Look, Dad, they have pajamas in his size with Scooby Doo on them. He loves to watch Scooby Doo."

"He is just like you were at his age; you never kept on the covers," said Howard. "Sounds like a good idea to me."

Now Andrew was not sure what to buy his little sister, Susan.

"I know!" he shouted as though a light had just come on in his head. "She is always singing, so how about a karaoke machine?"

"That is a wonderful idea, but you must remember it is her karaoke machine," remarked Howard. "Actually, it sounds like a lot of fun. I believe it is more than you should spend, though, but since you can all sing with it, I will help you to pay for it."

"Thanks, Dad; you're the best. I can't wait to see her face when she opens it!" Andrew was so excited.

"Yes, it will be fun to watch her reaction when she sees it," said Howard. "Now what have you decided to buy your mother?"

"I don't know; she is tough to buy for," commented Andrew. "Her wallet looked ratty the other day when she pulled it out to pay for groceries."

"Well, then, how about a new wallet for her? What color would you buy? The handbags she uses in the winter are usually dark brown or black."

"I think black, but let's go and look at them," said Andrew. "Mom will take me to buy your gift in town next week, probably after school one day. Oh, I just remembered she wants a clipboard, too, to put by her big calendar."

"Oh my goodness, the refrigerator will fall over," Howard said.

"Can we buy one of those for her too, Dad?" asked Andrew.

"A refrigerator or a clipboard?" Howard asked.

Andrew laughed and said, "A clipboard."

"Sure, let's go look for one, and then we'll find your Mom and Susan. I will give her a call to meet us somewhere near here," said Howard.

I answered my cell phone knowing it was Howard. He didn't wait for me to say hello before he asked, "Kim, where are you? Can we meet at the front entrance of JC Penney?"

I held my nose and answered, "I am sorry, Kim does not have on her cell phone; may I take a message?"

After a long pause, he said, "Yes, please tell the 'parking attendant' that the rest of her party will be at the front entrance to JC Penney in just a few minutes."

"Thank you; she and Susan are watching minstrels sing at the other end of the mall at Sears, but I will give her that message."

"You're very funny," Howard said, and then he hung up. It was a very tiring day and we were all exhausted from getting up early and walking in the cold at the tree farm and then fighting the crowds and traffic at the mall. There is a good pizza place here at the mall. It will be pizza for dinner tonight, which always means deciding what kind of pizza to order. One likes this and one likes that. We figured two slices each times six people equals twelve slices minus three, because the baby does not eat pizza, and Susan eats only one slice. Howard ended by buying two medium pizzas, one plain cheese and the other with mushrooms and pepperoni.

"Can we get a Hawaiian pizza again, Dad?" asked Andrew.

"Sure, said Howard, "but not tonight. It *was* good when we bought it before, with the ham and pineapple on it. You know, Andrew, on second thought, I just might buy that too."

"You go, Dad," laughed Andrew.

Howard bought three medium pizzas.

"Now to find your mother and sister," said Howard. "I do not know what is taking them so long. Here they come."

When we were close enough to speak, Howard said, "I bought three different pizzas in here. We will have to warm them some when we get home, but at least we have dinner with us."

"Thanks, honey," I said. "We were listening to the minstrels and looking in the store windows. We knew you would be a while ordering the pizzas." "I told Susan, you know your Daddy loves those pizzas here at the mall. I am sure he will buy some to take home."

⋆ ⋆ ⋆

While we were at the mall, Katie was at home taking good care of her baby brother. The floor was covered with toys. They were sitting on the floor playing with blocks and trucks. She is a good daughter. Kevin is a handsome little baby. Andrew and Susan look a lot like me, with straight, light-colored hair, but not Kevin and Katie. He is definitely Howard's son, and Katie his daughter. They both have dark hair, bright brown eyes, long legs, and sharp features. Howard has that granite jaw that looks so masculine; he's my handsome husband.

"It looks like you two have been busy," I said as Kevin crawled to me when we walked in the door, but I noticed he was saying "da-da-da" instead of "ma-ma."

"When are you going to start saying ma-ma?" I asked as I picked him up and gave him a hug. Turning to my daughter, I said, "Thank you, Katie, for watching Kevin while we were gone. Here is twenty dollars for you to use when you go to the mall."

"Thanks, Mom; he was good," Katie replied.

The phone rang and I answered it. It was Margaret. "Hi, Mom; yeah, come on over. Prefect timing—we brought home pizzas for dinner."

A little while later, we heard all the kids shout, "Hi, Grand-mom!" Margaret bustled in the door and sat down to eat with us. The kids wanted to tell her about their shopping day in the mall. Mom-Mom listened attentively, and then she said, "I want to tell you where I went Christmas shopping when I was a little girl.

My parents and my brother Edward and I lived outside of Philadelphia, Pennsylvania. Before Christmas, my mother would take my brother and me to the city to see the Christmas decorations and Santa Claus. In those days, there were big department stores in downtown Philly. Philly is a short name for Philadelphia. One store at that time was Snellenburg's. Another one was the John Wanamaker Store. This one had a golden eagle statue in the grand court, and in the balcony was a grand organ. Before and during the holidays, there was a light show. Everyone wanted to see and hear this beautiful performance. The announcer for the light show was John Facenda from WCAU-TV in Philadelphia. The light show, the organ, and the eagle are still there, but now the store is called Macy's. Wanamaker's had a Christmas Colonial Village, too. Now it is in the Please Touch Museum in Fairmont Park."

"On Thanksgiving, sometimes we would go into the city to watch the Gimbel's Thanksgiving Day Parade. We could watch it on television, too, just as we can do today. Now it is called the 6abc/Dunkin' Donuts Philadelphia Thanksgiving Day Parade. Santa and Mrs. Claus would ride in the sleigh at the end of the parade, and at exactly twelve o'clock noon when the parade ended, Santa Claus would climb a long fireman's ladder to a fifth-floor window of Gimbel's Department Store."

"When you went from floor to floor in the department stores, you either used a narrow escalator or you would ride up and down on the elevator. The elevator had an elevator attendant. He was the person who operated the elevator to the floor you wanted. If you started at the first floor, he might say, 'First floor cosmetics, millinery, which is ladies' hats; second floor ladies' clothing and lingerie; third floor men's haberdashery and suits; fourth floor shoes and coats; fifth floor, toys.' The salespeople were very familiar with the department they worked in and could answer all of your questions. The saleswomen always wore dresses, and the men wore neckties. It was not like today when there is no one in the department to assist you, or if someone is there, he or she does not know anything about the department. The salesclerks today are of no help at all."

"What is a habernasry?" asked Andrew, mispronouncing this unfamiliar word.

"Haberdashery is men's underclothing, such as pajamas and underwear," Margaret said.

"Strawbridge and Clothier later became just Strawbridge's. This store always had a Dickens Christmas Village."

"The story, book, and doll of Rudolph the Red-nosed reindeer were promotional items for the Montgomery Ward store. The singing cowboy, Gene Autry, sang that song, and of course, the story and the song are still Christmas classics today."

"I think one of my mother's favorite stores was Lit Brothers. There was a Lit Brothers in Philadelphia and a smaller one in Camden, New Jersey right across the bridge. Lit Brothers had a discount basement and animated dolls in the windows. Mother used to buy a five-pound tin of Christmas candy from them, and it was very good. The Lit Brothers building is still in Philadelphia, and I believe the store's name is now Ross. In the 1940s and 1950s, men and women wore hats, and on the side of the Lit Brothers building, there is still a saying on the wall that reads *Hats Trimmed Free of Charge*."

"What does that mean?" inquired Katie.

"*Hats Trimmed Free of Charge* meant that hats could be styled with a certain color headband or feather or maybe a flower, depending what the customer liked and there would be no charge for this service," Margaret answered.

"We would take a bus to Wanamaker's and have lunch in the restaurant there called the Crystal Tea Room, and if I can remember correctly, it was on the ninth floor. The restaurant was huge. We would stand in line to see Santa and tell him what we wanted for Christmas. My mother would always buy us a present from the city. One time she bought me a doll made in England and a Matchbox car set for my brother. We really loved this special day with our mother, and we have wonderful memories of the excitement of going downtown for Christmas shopping."

"Wow, Grand-mom, can we go there someday, too?" asked Andrew.

"Yeah, can we go, Grand-mom?" Susan asked. "And will you buy us presents like your mom did?"

"Maybe we can someday; it would be fun," Margaret answered. "Well, it is getting late, and I am tired. I am going home. I will call when I get into the apartment. Kisses and love to all; bye now," she said as she shut the door.

Andrew was so exhausted from his busy day of tree shopping, cutting down the tree, and walking through the mall. In order to bother his two sisters, he kept saying, "I bet you don't know what I bought you for Christmas!" Katie didn't mind, but he was driving Susan crazy. Being only six years old, she wanted to know. When bedtime came, he was the first to fall asleep. *Thank you, Lord,* I thought. Maybe we should keep him that busy every Saturday.

The winter nights are long. Howard is a sun and outdoor person. He cannot wait for spring and the longer days when the evenings stay light until 8:30 p.m. or later.

He likes to go outside after dinner in the spring and summer months. He plays with the dog or waters the flowers. Sometimes he and Andrew go for a bike ride. Sometimes he and I go for a walk and push the baby in his stroller. Susan likes to push the stroller, too. We just have to keep our eyes on her, because you never know where she will go. If we stop to speak to our neighbors, she is two blocks ahead of us.

The winter months give Howard rest time, or he plays games with the kids. Sometimes he will get crafty and make things in the basement or garage. Andrew likes to watch him, and I am glad he can learn from his father. Last year Howard taught him how to make a birdhouse. Occasionally, we even get a chance to cuddle a little on these cold winter nights. Of course, the kind of cuddling we usually do in this house is snuggling on the sofa with four children and two pets. It is hard to find time to be alone.

CHAPTER 8

On Sunday mornings, we attend church at the Skippack United Methodist Church. It is always a crazy morning trying to get there on time. I don't even remember what time Sunday school or church start. Either one of the children forgets something, or Kevin decides at that particular moment to burp up breakfast or dirty his diaper. My favorite is when Kevin, sitting in his highchair, sneezes into his food. Usually we both have to change then. It usually happens when he eats some kind of fruit that stains. He and the dog make quite a team. Kevin drops it and Midnight eats it. Yes, we call that teamwork!

We pulled into the parking lot at church and looked for a place to park. Having no luck with that, we pulled out onto the street and parked about two blocks from the church.

The church is old but beautiful, and it has awesome stained glass windows on both sides. The church itself is not big, but the church building has had many additions to accommodate various church functions. It has a large basement with a kitchen and banquet room for church dinners, as well as storage rooms, classrooms, and bathrooms.

The church family is just wonderful. The people seem to really care about one another. When you are sick, you receive a card and usually a phone call. People will bring dinners to your house. A few years back, Howard broke his leg. It was a very rough time for us. I had a two-year-old, a seven-year-old, and a ten-year-old. The fellows at the church came and mowed our grass for us. We were so shocked that they would do that, but we were very thankful.

We are blessed to attend this church. The church has many events, including the annual Christmas bazaar in the fellowship hall. We love it and either work at it or shop or both. Everyone is cordial and the gifts are so nice. Many are handmade. Lunch is available and there are things for the children to do and buy. The youth group helps to work in the nursery that day so the parents can either work or shop at the bazaar.

During the year, the church also runs a thrift shop. We donate clothes to them quite frequently. I love thrift stores. Of course, you have to watch what you buy, but you have to do that anywhere. Thrift shops are so interesting. You never know what you might find. When furnishing the kids' rooms, I found so many things that would add to their themes. When shopping at the thrift shop I get to converse with other church members, mostly women. A few women volunteer to run the thrift shop. They have it arranged by categories in four rooms. One room has clothes, shoes, and handbags. The next has seasonal merchandise, and of course, there are always many things for Christmas. Katie and I buy many things here to decorate the wreaths we make. That way we can keep the prices low. If we were to buy everything from the craft stores, we would have to charge double for the wreaths. In the next room are toys and books. The last room has knickknacks and household items. Sometimes people donate furniture to sell.

Occasionally, our church holds family dinners for the congregation, and everyone brings food from home. The church also provides the children a Halloween party at which we know they are safe. At Easter, we celebrate Holy Week, and there are special services leading up to Good Friday. On that day, the church does the Stations of the Cross. There are services throughout the day. On Palm Sunday weekend, which is the weekend prior to Good Friday, the church holds an Easter egg hunt for the little ones.

In the spring and summer, we have church-wide yard sales and our annual chicken barbecue picnic. The food is delicious. We have fun at the yard sale. If you want stuff, we sell it cheap, cheap, and cheaper! I think we have put a price tag on everything but the pastor. He is so much fun and a good sport. Last year he sat at the dunk tank. It was so hot that day that he did not mind being dunked repeatedly.

It seems every year this day is the hottest. One year we had a fast thunderstorm blow through. It poured and the wind blew hard. We had to wipe off all the seats and tables for the barbeque. Everyone was trying to cover things or hold them down. The covers on the tents were flapping in the breeze. Everyone was laughing as they tried to keep things from blowing away.

This weekend is the church Christmas bazaar. We donated items for the white elephant table. I told the children they were not allowed to buy back anything they donated. When they were younger, we would have yard sales in our yard, and they would take their stuff back into the house!

Earlier in the year, Katie and I made wreaths to sell for the church. Our wreaths have various themes, such as the manger scene, the Holy Family, a sleigh, Santa Claus, and many more. We make crosses and Christmas trees for people to put on the graves of their loved ones. We keep the prices low so they will sell. We really enjoy doing this, and it benefits the church. Many of the churchwomen give us ribbons and decorative items to use for making the wreaths. We help them out with whatever they need, too. One lady takes old hymnals, folds back the pages, and puts heads on them, turning them into angels.

It is really fun to work and shop at the bazaar. We all try to wear holiday sweaters or pins, and we play Christmas music to add to the festive decorations. Outside vendors pay ten dollars for a table to sell their items. Ten dollars is cheap, as most places want twenty or thirty dollars. The bazaar features a fifty-fifty auction, a Chinese auction, a white elephant section, handmade ornaments, baked goods, jars with jellies, cakes, and soups in them, crocheted items, flowers, calendars, homemade candles, Christmas items, and much more. You can buy used books and magazines at very low prices.

On the Sunday before Christmas, Susan and Andrew will be in the church's Christmas program. Susan will sing "Away in a Manger," and Andrew will recite a portion of scripture from the Christmas story from the book of Luke.

He will be a shepherd wearing a traditional bathrobe. He is rather shy, but Susan is a natural performer.

"Andrew, what will you recite for the Christmas program?" I asked.

"And there were shepherds living out in the fields nearby, keeping watch over their flocks by night. An angel of the Lord appeared to them, and the glory of the Lord shone around them, and they were terrified—Luke 2: 8-9."

"Very good," I said.

When we were driving home from the Christmas bazaar, Katie asked, "Mom, we forgot to do the Advent wreath for the dining-room table centerpiece."

"Oh yes, can you get the candles and everything for it? We can do that after lunch," I said.

Advent means"to come."

It is the time to prepare for God's greatest gift, the birth of Jesus Christ.

The Advent wreath was first used by the Protestants in Germany. The circle represents God's love, which is never ending. The evergreens symbolize the hope of eternal life. The four purple or blue candles represent the four weeks of Advent, during which a candle is lit each Sunday. The white candle is the Christ candle, and is placed in the center of the ring. It is lit on Christmas Eve or Christmas Day.

The candles symbolize hope, love, joy, and peace. This is to prepare our hearts and minds for the birth of our Savior, Jesus Christ.

It is only three weeks until Christmas and the cards are finished, and I actually remembered to included school photos in them. Katie, Susan, and I have been busy baking cookies. The girls are really a big help. Andrew and Howard are not! I told them they could eat the broken chocolate chip cookies. It is amazing that we only have about a dozen cookies out of five dozen cookies that are not broken! I do have to admit they are best when right from the oven. They sneak into the kitchen, thinking we do not see them, and then they break a cookie and sneak out.

"Hey, get out of here!" Susan yelled.

"Yeah guys, we see you eating those cookies," said Katie.

"I am amazed at how many are broken," I said as I gave them a wry look.

"These cookies are great," said Andrew.

"Here comes Grand-mom to help bake cookies!" yelled Susan.

"Are we done yet?" asked Margaret when she breezed into the kitchen. "How does that cookie taste?" She asked Kevin.

Kevin is in his highchair eating a cookie. He has chocolate everywhere.

"Aren't you going to kiss the baby, Mom?" I said as I laughed.

Margaret answered, "Yes, but later; he seems to be enjoying the cookie."

"Oh, the kitchen is covered in baking stuff and cookies, lots of cookies. We have baked all day. We made some of the batters yesterday so we could start baking early this morning."

"Do you want another cookie, honey?" Margaret asked him. Of course, he nodded his head yes and said, "Ma-ma."

"What did he say?" I asked. "Did my little boy say ma-ma? My goodness, I could eat you up; you are so delicious," I said to him as I kissed him. "Let's wash your hands and face." He was not happy about having his face washed.

The kitchen looked like a disaster had hit. Flour, sugar, eggshells, and chocolate chips were everywhere. We had fun baking, though, and we will clean up later. I decided to do a cookie exchange with other mothers, and I am quite excited about it. There are fifteen women in the cookie swap, so each of us bakes fifteen dozen of our favorite cookie. I will keep one dozen and the other fourteen women will each take a dozen. We decided this year to bake two dozen cookies for each mom. It sounds like a lot, but it really isn't. Of course, by the time everyone eats those "broken" cookies, it never looks like we have that many. It is fun for the family to participate, and when company visits over the holidays, we have two dozen of fifteen different kinds of cookies to serve. The cookies are delicious and beautifully decorated. We even made Springerles(a special German picture cookie that is rolled and has a stamp imprint). The Springerles take some time. They have a mild anise taste. This cookie is very expensive to buy at the bakery.

Suddenly I hear Kevin giggling. When I look around to see him, he is giving the dog his cookies and the dog is licking his hands to get all the cookie crumbs.

"What are you doing, little boy?" I asked. "We do not have to look far for the dog."

"Mommy, we made all these cookies, but we forgot one kind," said Susan.

"What kind is that, honey?" I asked. "With all these different cookies, I can't believe we missed one kind. I am up to my ears in cookie crumbs!"

"Gingerbread! Can we make gingerbread men with icing for the clothes and raisins for the eyes and buttons?" asked Susan.

"Yes, ok, but are you going to help me?" I asked.

"Yes, Mommy, I will get the raisins," said Susan. The cookie cutter I use for the gingerbread man was my grand mother's. It brings back wonderful memories of baking cookies with her, and with my mother and sister. We loved baking the gingerbread cookies, but then no one ate them. We did enjoy decorating them.

"Do you want the icing on them, too?" I asked.

"Oh, yes," she answered.

Now for the mystery—will anyone eat them?

We were all tired at the end of this day and weekend, but it was so much fun and created even more memories for our family. Everyone helped; even little Susan.

CHAPTER 9

We placed the manger stable with Mary, Joseph, and the animals in our living room. We did not have the angel, shepherds, wise men, or baby Jesus in the manger yet.

Susan asked me, "Why don't we put baby Jesus in the manger now? He is what Christmas is all about, Mommy."

I smiled and gently took her face in my hands and kissed her cheek. "Yes, dear, you are so right. Remember, we put baby Jesus into his little bed of hay and blankets on Christmas Eve. You children take turns, and I believe this year is your turn. And whose turn is it to help Daddy put the star on the top of the tree?"

"I don't 'member," answered Susan.

"I think it is Kevin's turn," I said. "You can help me put the wise men and the star to the side," I said.

"Why?" she asked. "You're not gonna put them in the manger?"

"No, we are not going to put them in the manger," I said, "Because the wise men followed the star, and they came from far away, so they did not see the baby Jesus in the stable, but in a house when he was about two years old. We will add the angel and the shepherds to the manger scene on Christmas Eve."

"I like the angel, Mommy. She is so pretty. Can we see angels, or just this one?" questioned Susan.

"Susan," I said softly, "I believe we do have angels around us every day to protect and guide us. Maybe we cannot see them, but I believe angels come to us in the way of friends. Friends are the people who stay near us to love us, comfort us, and protect us when other people walk out and leave us."

"But, where are their wings?" Susan wondered.

"I do not really know; but perhaps we cannot see their wings here on earth, but we will when we go to heaven." My explanation seemed enough for now, and she was content.

Today we will decorate the tree. We always decorate it about a week or two before Christmas. Things are just too busy to wait until closer to Christmas. Each child gets to put on his or her new ornaments. We always have Christmas music or movies playing, or we sing Christmas carols or hymns.

"Katie, could you make us all a cup of hot chocolate? I bought all the different flavors. This room is a bit chilly." Andrew is helping Howard situate the tree in its stand, and I will help with the lights. Lights and tinsel—the two are my nemesis. The doorbell rang. It is our friend, Linda, and her grandchildren, Lori, Cole, and Jonathan, asking if we would like to go to the general store for ice cream.

"Have I got a deal for you!" I teased. "If you help us with the ornaments and putting on a little tinsel, we will be done decorating sooner and could go with you. Does that sound like fun?"

"Ok," they said and they took off their coats and the tree trimming began. Andrew led us in singing, "I want a hippopotamus for Christmas, only a hippopotamus will do...." We shared many laughs with that song. Even Kevin was jumping up and down in his bouncy chair laughing. Kevin is now crawling and standing. Soon he will be walking. The whole time we are singing, he claps his little hands and says "da-da-da" and blows bubbles. Andrew plays hide and seek with him, and every time he pokes his head out, Kevin just laughs and laughs. I am waiting to hear ma-ma-ma again, but no such luck. I look at him and realize that he is our last baby. I just love the ages between one and three years. Sure, it is a demanding time for a mother, but it is my favorite time. That first year of life is so amazing! You hold that brand new helpless infant in your arms. You watch him as his eyes follow your voice. Soon he will coo and smile. On his first birthday, you are in awe of the milestones he has accomplished; he has gone from a newborn infant to a little person walking and trying to talk.

Then the terrible twos and threes come along. Despite what so many parents say about these two years, I think they are fun, because everything is new and exciting to your growing toddler. When he walks and suddenly falls down, he gives you a look that says, *What happened? I was up just a minute ago; what am I doing sitting on the floor?* Toddlers' expressions are priceless. You watch as they lose their baby-fat and become little children. Everything about them is amazing.

I scooped Kevin up in my arms and said, "You are growing too quickly, little boy. Let me get the camera and take some pictures of us decorating the tree." I started to sing *This Little Light of Mine.* When I got to the part that says, "Don't let Satan blow it out," I shook my head no and pretended to blow out the candle, which was my finger. Kevin laughed and mimicked me by spitting and puffing at his little finger while shaking his head no. Everyone was singing and laughing.

Thank you, Lord, for laughter, happiness, and babies.

I put Kevin on the floor and went to get the camera. When I returned I asked Katie, "Where is Kevin?"

"Mom, he was just here. He is not under the tree or in the ornaments, is he?" Katie laughed. Suddenly we saw a trail of toilet tissue going down the hallway. He likes to pull the tissue off the roll and then crawl away very quickly with it. Katie went to get him. She said, "I am going to get you, Kevin! Here I come, Kevin." The closer she came, the faster he crawled and giggled. Katie took the toilet tissue and wrapped it around him, and I had to take a photo—he was so cute.

"Mom, he looks like a mummy."

I only said, "It is a shame that child has no toys and has to play with toilet tissue!"

Ok, here comes trouble, the cat. Kit-Kat is hiding in the Christmas boxes. Next thing we know, the cat is batting balls across the floor. Kevin cannot stop laughing. Then Andrew is on the floor with Midnight. Midnight decides to be near Kevin and just sit. Kevin crawls over to the sleigh we have by the fireplace. He takes the stuffed toys out of the little sleigh and climbs inside. Two seconds later, he is out and on the crawl again. Andrew is right behind him on his hands and knees.

Last year Susan gave me a glitter pinecone she made in kindergarten. The handmade ornaments are my most precious ones. This year she made a little school-girl ornament since she is in first grade. Howard gave me a baby photo-frame ornament with Kevin's picture in it. Katie bought a dainty angel with hair like silk. It looks so fragile. Andrew wanted a soccer ball ornament, but he insisted we buy a dog bone-shaped ornament with Midnight's name written on it, and an ornament for Kit-Kat. For the cat, he chose one that was a cat with bird feathers in its mouth and *What bird?* written on it. I still put some of my parent's ornaments on the tree, high enough to keep them from being broken by animals and little fingers, and the ones Howard gave me for each baby. Howard and I both put on the one given to us for our first Christmas as husband and wife.

When we finished the tree and cleaned the mess, there on the floor was Midnight with little Kevin sleeping with his head on the dog. It was another perfect Kodak moment.

Our sixteen-year marriage has been blessed with love and affection. We both wanted children and pets. Not only are we lovers; we are best friends, too. We like simple things, and we still hold hands when we can. Usually, we are holding on to little hands. We laugh and try not to take ourselves too seriously. The children won't let us! Sometimes we may disagree, but we never fight. We have been blessed four times with healthy wonderful children. We thank God every day for everything.

This is the day the Lord has made. We will rejoice and be glad in it.

Psalm 118:24 (NIV)

Corrie Ten Boon, the author of *The Hiding Place*, wrote in her book that her sister, Betsie, gave thanks for the fleas where they slept in the concentration camp. Corrie disagreed with her saying that her sister had gone too far in thanking God for these awful fleas. Corrie realized later it was because of the fleas that the soldiers did not want to go into their barracks.. That way they could pray to God for each other.

Betsie said, "God says to give thanks in all circumstances, not just in pleasant circumstances. Fleas are part of this place where God has put us."

It was hell on earth for them, but they were faithful to God's word.

In all things, give thanks.

Children need discipline in order to know right from wrong. In today's world, parents are discouraged from correcting their children for some odd reason, and if we do, we may find the police on our doorstep. Abuse is wrong, but we need to discipline our children to teach them morals and boundaries. In many homes today, children say, "Oh, my parents are my best friends." The problem is the parents are trying to be the teenagers in the way they dress and act, and the teenagers are trying to be like the parents, drinking and smoking. Many parents are enablers and allow their children to drink, smoke, or do drugs. Actually, the parents and the teenagers are "hanging out" together. This is why parents need to be parents, and they need to remember that teenagers are still kids who need guidance and direction.

You may have a wonderful relationship with your daughter or son, but that is just that: she is your daughter, and he is your son. They are not your buddies. They need to know right from wrong, and they need to experience the consequences of their actions. Children need to learn respect and to show respect. They need to feel unconditional love and know that they are always *safe* in their home. As they grow older, they need to learn responsibility. When they are married and have their own children, then you can be buddies with them. Until then, you are to discipline them, because you are the parent and he or she is your child. Your children will always be your babies no matter how old they are.

Train a child in the way he should go, and when he is old he will not turn from it.

Proverbs 22:6 (NIV)

CHAPTER 10

The elementary school Christmas program was this morning. I was so glad that Howard could be with me. When he told Susan he could be at her program, she gave him a love-lock hug, or her tight hug as she calls it. She was so happy. Howard's mother, Margaret, was meeting us in the school parking lot at 9:40 a.m. so that we could get good seats together. We were so happy that she could join us. We did not tell Susan because we wanted her to be surprised when she saw her grandmother in the audience. We hoped Kevin would sleep through the entire program; no such luck. He slept some and then woke up and started to cry. Regrettably, I missed some of Susan's program because I had to take him out. Howard said she sang her heart out. The girls wore either red or green skirts or pants and a Christmas sweater, and the boys did the same, except they wore only pants, of course. There were refreshments afterward in the back of the room. It was nice to spend a little time with the children after the program.

First the kindergarten children performed. These little ones are my favorites. It is so comical to watch them. Usually one cries or walks in the opposite direction. Sometimes one will walk to the front of the stage and wave, or walk off the stage. Their teachers are on the sides of the stage to help and guide them so these little ones constantly watch them. If dancing is involved, it is quite hysterical. They are so busy watching the teachers that they forget their steps, or they do the ones they enjoy over and over again. When the audience claps, so do they. It is enchanting to watch, as these children will never be this little again. When their performance is over, they line up and walk off the stage like little penguins.

Next to go on stage were the first graders. Susan loves school, so she has no problem being on stage or in front of an audience. She is always singing and performing at home for us. Susan spotted us in the audience and showed us a big smile. Howard took some photos. They are all so cute. The girls' slips are showing and the boys shirttails are hanging out. Their hair is uncombed, food is on their faces, and their shoes are untied. They forget the words, but they remember to shout or clap at just the right time. When they notice their parents, siblings, or maybe even their grandparents in the audience, they smile from ear to ear. Susan sang her solo, "All I Want for Christmas Is My Two Front Teeth," and yes, she is now missing both of her front teeth.

After the school day ended at two o'clock in the afternoon, the children in the elementary school were invited to shop at the Christmas store. Margaret said she had to leave to run her errands in order to be home before dark. Kevin quieted down and fell asleep, so I stayed to help by wrapping gifts for the children. The kids get so excited. One little boy told me that he had to buy a New Hampshire road map for his daddy because his mommy says that Daddy is always lost and refuses to ask for directions! Have I heard this before? The children are so funny. A little girl said to me that she has to buy the teapot for her mommy, because when Mommy makes a cup of tea, that string and tag are always hanging out of her cup. When she buys the teapot, Mommy can hide the teabag in there so no one will see the string and tag.

Susan showed me what she bought for her daddy.

"Oh, Susan, your dad will love this," I said. She had chosen a tie and tie tack for Howard.

I remember when Andrew was in first grade. He came in the front door, ran through the house and into his bedroom, slamming the door. I could hear him moving things around in his room and closet as he hid our secret presents. I sat there reminiscing about the Christmas school programs we had when I was a child. We actually sang Christmas songs that had to do with the Christ child, such as, "Away in a Manger" and "Oh Little Town of Bethlehem." Now the schools are not to let the children sing religious songs. It may offend only one or two persons, but the other fifty people may want to sing those traditional songs. Now we hear "Jingle Bells" and "Have a Holly Jolly Christmas" in the school program. Nice holiday songs, very cheerful, but what do they have to do with the Christ of Christmas? This is similar to how Happy Holidays is on everything from Christmas cards to advertisements instead of Merry Christmas.

When my generation was in elementary school, we stood with our hands over our hearts and said the Pledge of Alliance to the flag of the United States of America. We sang a patriotic song and we read something from the Bible. Isn't it ironic that our children cannot read the Bible in school where they are growing and learning, but they are allowed to read the Bible in jail later in life? Maybe, just maybe this is because they were not allowed to read a Bible earlier in school.

Everyone needs to stand and show respect for our flag and our country. Men and women today are dying to defend both. Children need to know the words to our national anthem, and they should know what those words mean. We have to stand up for our service members, our flag, and our country, or someday we may be singing a different song. I never want that to happen to our great country, the United States of America.

Blessed is the nation whose God is the Lord.

Psalm 33:12 (NIV)

Kevin and I arrived home about four o'clock. Since the day was cloudy it seemed to be getting darker earlier this evening. Howard got home earlier, too, so we could eat and go out tonight.

"This evening we have a surprise for you, Susan and Kevin," Howard announced. "What have we not done yet this year that we have to do before Christmas?"

"Go see Santa Claus!" Susan screamed. "I don't need a list 'cause I mem-ized everything I want."

"I am sure you did." Howard laughed.

On the way to Bauer's General Store to see Santa, Susan asked, "Do you remember the song we were learning in church, Mommy?"

"Yes, dear, I believe it was 'Come to the Manger'."

"I like it, Mommy. Do you remember all the words?"

"Not all of them. If it is not too late when we get home, I will find the words and we will sing it together before bedtime, ok?"

"Ok, Mommy," she replied in her sweet little voice.

Bauer's General Store was crowded, but not as bad as I had imagined. Luckily, we came on a school night. Kevin was not exactly happy on Santa's knee, but he did not cry. Instead, it was quite funny, because he just stared at Santa's beard and hat. His big, brown eyes were examining this different person holding him. Susan was right; she did memorize her list, and did not miss a beat telling Santa everything she wanted. Then, to our surprise, when she got to the end of her list, she asked Santa to please remember the poor children and bring gifts to them, but not just toys. She wanted them to have new clothes and food to eat. I think Santa was surprised, and he thanked her for thinking of other children.

"Susan, that was very nice what you asked Santa," I said. "Maybe next time we go to town we can purchase a couple of toys to add to the Toys for Tots donation box here in the general store. Does that sound like a good idea to you?"

"Oh yes, I can help you pick them out," answered Susan.

Good idea, I thought, *but where is my head? I will never get her away from the toys! Oh well, it is a good deed and for a good cause.*

The general store has so many different things to look at or buy for Christmas. I wanted to look, but tomorrow is a school day, so we saw Santa and left. I thought to myself, *I'll be back!*

When we finally arrived home, I found the words to "Come to the Manger" so, as promised, we sang the song before bed. It was my special time with my daughter.

Come, come, come to the manger
Children, come to the children's King
Sing, sing,
Chorus of angels,
Stars of morning, over Bethlehem sing.
He lies 'mid the beasts of the stall,
Who is Maker and Lord of us all
The wintry wind blows cold and dreary
See, He weeps, the world is weary
Lord, have pity and mercy on me.
Come, come
Come to the manger.
Author Unknown

CHAPTER 11

Since this is Kevin's first Christmas and we do not expect to have more children, we had a family photo taken as a surprise for my sister, my father, and Howard's mother. What were we thinking? Andrew and Susan wanted the cat and dog in the photo, too. "But, they are family, too," they exclaimed. I told them no. Trying to get four children to cooperate is more than enough to cope with; but easy-going Howard said that the animals could be in the picture. I truly do not think he gave this picture-taking event much thought.

First Andrew, who had Kit-Kat in his arms, put down the cat. Kit-Kat promptly ran off and hid behind the photo screen. Next he was behind the camera stands. Then he ran behind the photo screen again. Help!

"Please pick up the cat, Andrew," I said firmly.

Katie was complaining that Midnight got dog hair on her outfit and that no one remembered to bring a sticky roller to clean the hair from our clothes. Susan was picking her nose because she is congested. Andrew was crawling under the photo screen looking for the cat. Midnight was licking her rear end.

"Mom, I popped a button," Katie said.

"Just cover it up somehow," I said.

"Look, Dad," Andrew announced as he put on reindeer antlers.

"No, you cannot wear those today for this picture," Howard snapped.

This seemed like the appropriate time for Kevin to wet his diaper and decide to cry. Right on schedule, he did just that.

Midnight started barking when she heard other customers coming in the front door of the shop.

"Get out of the way, Andrew; I can't see the picture lady!" Susan yelled.

"Stop touching me!" Andrew snapped.

"Don't pull my hair," Susan retorted.

"I'll get you when we get home," warned Andrew.

"Hey, knock it off, all of you," yelled Howard. "Let's all smile for some nice pictures. Remember, these are going to be gifts, and we don't want to look bad or mad."

"Andrew, you hold the dog, and Katie, you hold the cat. Susan, get over here with Kevin," said Howard.

"Am I still smiling?" I whispered to Howard.

"Don't get me laughing, Kim," Howard muttered, but it made him smile.

"Did the photographer say smile or scream?"

"Is she still here, or did she run out to escape?"

I believe she took the rest of the day off after our family left. Somehow, this well trained, professional photographer captured great shots, and we all look happy. Amazingly, no animals were looking the other way, no children were fighting, and neither parent had that *why did we have four children?* look. Thankfully, no photographers were injured during this photo shoot!

"Gee, Kevin, maybe when you are eighteen we will have another family photo taken," I growled when we were heading home in the car.

Today was cold, but I decided it was a nice, bright, sunny day to do a little shopping in town. So, after the photo shoot, the children went with me so they could buy a few things they might want as gifts. I put Kevin in his car seat and off we went. We enjoyed walking through town. Kevin is good in his stroller. Of course, he is not thrilled about the seatbelt on him, but that is too bad.

About a month ago, I was in the drug store looking at greeting cards, and I had Kevin in the stroller in front of me. I turned around to look at him, and that fast he was gone, not in his stroller. Well, I was absolutely beside myself with fear. I quickly looked around, but I saw no one near us, and then I heard a giggle. I grabbed the stroller and went to the end of the aisle. There he was crawling as quickly as he could and giggling as loudly as he could. He wanted me to chase him. A couple other customers saw us and started to laugh. I then felt much better. I scooped him up and hugged him, and smiled as they watched me. I looked at them and made the comment, "Guess who is getting a seat belt installed in his stroller?" That day I bought one while we were out, and Howard connected it to the stroller. At first, Kevin hated it. He pulled on it and screamed like we were holding him down, but the seat belt is there for keeps. I was terrified that day when I thought I'd lost him, and now I know he is secure and safe. Howard calls him the *little prisoner.*

We had fun going in and out of the shops in Skippack. Susan mainly came along for the ride, but Andrew still had to buy gifts for his father, grandparents, and Aunt Jeanette. Katie still had quite a few things to buy. The Candy Cupboard had all the decorated Christmas candy so, of course, we made a stop in there. We were definitely acting like kids in a candy store.

I said, "The candy is decorated so prettily that you almost do not want to bite into it."

"I do," Andrew said as he gulped down a piece of chocolate.

"Mommy, we have to see the dog and cat stuff," said Susan.

"Ok, we will go there next, but how can I leave all this wonderful chocolate?" After making our purchase, we took off to the pet shop.

By the time we left the Pitter-Patter Paw Pet Place, the cat and dog each had Christmas hats as well as their own little gifts: baked dog biscuits, a holiday bandana, and a squeak toy for Midnight; a holiday collar and a little wind-up mouse for Kit-Kat. For the whole family, I bought a car decal with a paw print design that reads, *Who adopted who?*

We saved the general store for last. The children always seem to get lost in there. Of course, the Bauers love them and spoil them every time they go in there.

This will be Kevin's first Christmas, so naturally we wanted a first Christmas ornament for him. Well, with three other children helping me decide, he now has three ornaments. The ornaments were too cute, too many, and there was just too much variety, so now we had to have more than one ornaments labeled that said Baby Boy's First Christmas, Baby's 1st Christmas, and Kevin's First Christmas.

"Andrew, what do you have?" I asked.

Laughing, he said, "Look, Mom, it is a head, and you spin it around, and the face is happy on one side and scary on the other." He loved it, and I thought it was terrible.

"Is that a present for one of your friends or yourself?" I asked. "It is so ugly; please tell me it is for one of your friends."

"Yeah, I am going to buy it for RJ; he will love it."

"Good, that way I won't have to see it," I said. "While we are here we have to buy two toys for the Toys for Tots donation box located in the back of the store."

I recognized the salesclerk behind the cash register. "Hi, Lenora Lee, how are you?" I asked. I had not seen her since the day Mildred and I had taken her shopping, and we had stopped in here so that she could speak with Mr. Bauer about a job.

"Oh, hi Kim, thank you so much for the other day—I mean the shopping and lunch. I really enjoy working here, and Mr.and Mrs. Bauer let my children come here after school so they can do their homework and I do not have to pay for a sitter. So far the children have behaved."

"Oh, you have nice kids," I said. "We told you the Bauers are good people."

"This store is so big and has just about everything. I am still learning!" Lorena Lee said.

"I think you will be learning for a long time. I have come in here for ten years and still cannot find everything," I said with a wry smile. "I love the things for Christmas. The items are interesting and different, and priced so reasonably. There is a nice selection of ornaments and Christmas craft pieces." While the kids were looking about the store, I thought I'd take the opportunity to speak a little more personally with Lenora Lee.

"How are things for you?" I asked.

"Good," she answered." I have started divorce proceedings. I hated doing it, but I cannot live like that or have my children subject to the drinking and abuse."

"You did the right thing; we will talk later. More people are coming through the door. Have a good evening," I said to her cheerily, and we started to leave.

"I hope you and the children can visit us during the holidays," Lenora Lee said as we were walking out the door.

"Thank you!" I called out. "That would be very nice. We'll see if our schedule permits."

* * *

I am so glad we have a large dining area, because during the holidays we really fill the room. Besides the six of us, Howard's mother will be here. Howard's father died two years ago. His mother lives near us in a senior complex. It seems to be a nice community. It is clean and the people are friendly. They have many activities in which she participates: bingo, day bus trips, crafts, movies, and luncheons just to name a few. We are thankful she still drives with no problems. We call her every other day and see her every week. She loves to babysit little Kevin for me. He enjoys staying with his Mom-Mom. She has a car seat in her car and loves to show him off to her friends and neighbors. When she takes him out for the day, we can be sure that he will come home with a new toy, stuffed animal, or item of clothing. Howard always teases her and says, "You never bought me all that stuff when I was a baby!"

"Oh now, you know you were spoiled; you were an only child," Margaret commented back to him. "You could do no wrong in your father's eyes; my son this and my son that," she said. "Your father was a good man," as she hid the tears from her eyes.

My father and sister will join us from New Jersey. They will drive here on December 23, so they will be here for the Christmas Eve church service, the live nativity, and Christmas Day. They will return home early the following week. The girls will sleep in the family room on the pullout sofa, and Andrew will sleep in his sleeping bag on the floor, loving every minute of it. He would always sleep in his sleeping bag if we let him. This way Grand-mom Margaret and Aunt Jeanette will have beds in one room, and Grand-pop will be in the other room. We will move Kevin and his crib into our room so that if he cries, he won't wake his Grand-pop.

My sister, Jeanette, is a second-grade school teacher. She is five years my senior. I am taller and thinner, but she has the beautiful wavy hair. My hair was always straight. She was engaged once, but the marriage plans ended and she just kept going, but she never married. Who knows? Maybe someday wedding bells will ring for her. I always thought it sad, because she would have made a loving mother. She is a blessing in the way she takes such good care of our father. They live together so she can help him with laundry, shopping, cleaning, and doctor appointments. Our dad, however, is very independent. He is sixty-five years old, but to look at him you would think he is not a day over fifty-five. He takes wonderful care of himself. He tries to eat healthy, exercises every day, sees his doctor regularly, and sleeps well. He is one of those "early to bed, early to rise, makes a man healthy, wealthy, and wise" people. There must be something to that old saying, because Dad looks great. He looks better than Howard and I do.

Dad and Jeanette still live in the same old house we grew up in, better known as home. It is a two-story house with a low ceiling basement and a very small attic. The living room and dining room both have bay windows. Mother and Daddy always put the Christmas tree in the living room window and her plants, African violets, were in the dining room window. When we were young there were French doors between the living room and dining room, but Mother always said they were in the way, so Daddy took them down.

There is also a small bedroom with an adjoining bathroom, a small kitchen, and a laundry room on the first floor. The upstairs has three bedrooms and one bathroom. Since the house is old, the bathroom is large. At one time, we are sure it was another bedroom. In the front of the house is a screened porch that extends from one side of the house to the other. We spent many fun times on that screened porch swinging on the glider and playing games. In the summer, it was delightful to sit out there. The house used to have asbestos shingles, but many years ago Daddy had them covered with aluminum siding.

Mother and Daddy always had beautiful flowers and a small garden. I remember picking tomatoes and strawberries as a young girl. The roses in the garden were just lovely. Mother and Daddy were so generous to everyone they visited. They would take a bouquet of flowers or a container of strawberries or something else from the garden when they visited. Our mother would always say, "Don't say thank you for the flowers or they will wilt." The yard is still maintained, but there is not much of a garden anymore. They do grow tomatoes and still have some flowering trees.

The one tree I remember so well is the magnolia tree they brought home with them from the south. Mother did not know if it would survive in the north. The tree grew very tall, and each year it had the biggest, most beautiful blooms. Daddy and Mother could grow anything. The holly tree still has berries and the azaleas always bloom in the front yard during the spring. Along the sidewalk in the backyard are the daffodils. Every time I see daffodils, I think of our daddy.

It is so wonderful that God gives us memories that are ours forever.
I have wonderful memories of my childhood.

Howard's father was not an old man when he was diagnosed with cancer. It was an awful time, but thankfully, he did not suffer long. We felt badly, because he never had the chance to see his youngest grandson, Kevin. He loved the grandchildren, and he would tell them stories of when he had to walk a mile to school in the deep snow with only torn shoes. He would tell them about his days as a little boy in grammar school. If the air raid siren sounded, the children were either to go under their desks or down into the basement and sit against the wall. This was around the time of the Korean War. Then there were the tales of when he had to eat all his food on his dinner plate before he could go out to play; otherwise, he would be punished and have to stay inside. If he had been misbehaving a lot at Christmastime, he would only get a piece of black coal in his Christmas stocking. That story scared the kids. It was funny as he went on and on with these stories, some of them fabricated, but the children loved him and would listen attentively.

Howard was an only child. When he married, he wanted a family. He knew the loneliness of not having brothers or sisters. He has some cousins, but the family is rather small.

My mother passed when Susan was just a baby. She suffered a massive heart attack. She, too, did not get to see Kevin. Her grandchildren were her world. Both sets of parents spoiled these children so much. When the children stayed with them for the weekend, they would let them misbehave and then send them home to us. At the same time, they would giggle and mumble under their breaths, “Payback! We hope your children are just like you.” This seemed odd to us, because of course, we thought we had been perfect in every way when we were children—ha!

Every year Howard’s parents would buy the children’s Easter outfits, and my parents would purchase their Christmas clothes. Jeanette bought the clothes this year. She sent them by UPS and they arrived about a week ago so the children would have them for Christmas Eve and Christmas Day. Actually, she had Katie pick out what she wanted, and then asked her to send a picture of it with the color, size, and where it could be purchased. It had to be exactly what Katie wanted. She is a teenager, you know. Andrew received a pair of brown pants with a shirt to match, and a brown and tan colored designer sports coat. He looks so grown up and handsome in it. It is funny, because when I call him handsome, he blushes and runs to his room. If I kiss him on the cheek, he hurriedly wipes it off. He is not to the age where he wants a girl to be near him, much less kiss him, and it even embarrasses him when I give him a peck on the cheek. He is only eleven, so hopefully his girl-chasing days are a long time away.

When it comes to buying Christmas clothes for the little ones, I just go crazy in their clothing departments. The clothes are so little and cute, and I just want to buy everything. Then I go into the little girls' section and just love the clothes for Susan. Of course, she already wants to pick out her own clothes, so that sometimes poses a problem. We do not always agree on what to buy. So really, I am glad my sister does this for me. Susan was sent a beautiful red velvet dress, very plain, with a white furry collar and cuffs. I fell in love with it. Jeanette must have purchased this dress in a children's designer shop. Our little guy is going to look ready for Christmas in his red and green one-piece that reads *Baby's First Christmas.* Howard and I do not often buy clothes for ourselves. I try to maintain my size ten, which means I can wear my holiday outfits for years.

Trying to keep the house clean is impossible at Christmas. Besides the usual dog hair, cat hair, baby toys, and animal toys, and there are decorations everywhere. It seems as though there are more children in the kitchen and house than usual. Who are all these people?

"Mom, can we have some of the pizza bites in the freezer?" asked Andrew.

"Sure," I said. "Just read the instructions; it is easy. Do not burn yourself, and clean up after yourselves. If not, everyone will have to go home."

"Mommy, can I hang the stars I made for the windows?" asked Susan. "Everyone will see them with the window candle lights."

"Yes, of course, you can. What beautiful stars you made," I said as I held them in my hands. Each star is on glitter paper with a shimmery cord attached to the outside for hanging it.

Kevin has developed a cold. It seemed not serious enough to see a doctor, but he still felt miserable, so I tried rocking him to sleep. I had medicine from before, so I gave him some. He is teething too. So far, he has two teeth that look so adorable in his pictures.

Katie had to buy gifts for all her friends and was planning a sleepover after Christmas. We don't mind. She has nice friends even though they do eat us out of house and home. They laugh and make noise, but they are really good girls, and they quiet down when told to. They help to clean afterward, too. The problem we have when the girls are here is Andrew. He is a typical younger brother who has to torment his sister and her friends the entire night. He scares them, teases them, follows them, or just drives them crazy. That's our boy!

Howard was hanging garland in the family room. I watch him for a minute and try to remember the next item on my list. Oh yes—we need the extra leaves in the large table and the tablecloths, too. This is holiday madness!

The doorbell rang and it was my neighbor, Nancy. "Hi, how are you?" she said cheerfully.

"I'm good," I said. "Come on in."

"Let me hold that sweet little boy," she said as she took Kevin in her arms.

"He is just not himself today, Nancy. He has a little cold and is possibly teething, so he is not happy."

"Oh, poor little guy. I hope he feels better. Do you need anything for him?" Nancy asked.

"I gave him some medicine. I really think he needs a nap. I was rocking him hoping he would fall asleep. Let me put him down for a nap. Hopefully, he will feel better when he awakens."

"Your tree always looks nice—big, but nice," commented Nancy.

"According to my husband, the word for the tree this year is *grand*," I told her.

"Your dining room, living room, and family room are always decorated lovely," said Nancy.

"Yes, but on Christmas Eve maybe, and especially on Christmas Day, everything is turned upside-down! But, I am happy we are parents and have a family."

"It's that way in every house on Christmas morning if you have children. You should see the mess two teenage girls and one ten-year-old boy can make, but I wouldn't want it any other way," replied Nancy.

"Nancy, you always know just what to say to make me laugh or feel better," I said.

"Mommy, can we string popcorn to put on the tree?" Susan asked.

We have not done that for a long time, so I said, "Yes, that would be fun. You get my sewing box so I can get a large needle and thread, and maybe Aunt Nancy can help pop the popcorn."

"Aunt Nancy, can I help string the popcorn and hang it?" It was Andrew running through the doorway.

"Of course, you can. I think we can use all the help we can get," exclaimed Nancy.

"Andrew, did your friends all go home?" I asked.

"Yes, Mom," he answered.

"When you bring in that many friends, please let me know who you have with you, ok?" I asked. "Sometimes I feel like a stranger in my own home."

"Okay, Mom," Andrew said.

To my neighbor, I said, "Thanks, Nancy; I knew you wouldn't mind popping the popcorn."

When I was a child, my parents always taught my sister and me to show respect to adults by calling them Mr., Mrs., or Miss before their name. If they were a family friend, we called them aunt or uncle as the children did with Nancy. We were never allowed to call them by their first name only. I believe it is disrespectful for children to call their parents by their first names. I went through hours of labor to have each one of these precious children, so I deserve and earned the right to be called either Mommy, Mom, or Mother.

Honor your mother and father.

Exodus 20:12 (NIV)

When I returned from putting Kevin down to sleep, I saw that Andrew, Susan, and Nancy were stringing and hanging popcorn already. The next thing we knew, Kit-Kat was smacking a piece of popcorn across the room. Then he saw the string, grabbed it, and took off into the other room. At this point Midnight was barking and chasing after the cat while the tree was tilting from the pull on the string. Andrew and Susan were hysterical with laughter and I was praying that the ornaments wouldn't break. *Zoom*—there went the cat with the dog not far behind. Suddenly they stopped, and the cat took off into another room and the dog stopped to eat the popcorn.

I laughingly said, "Maybe this wasn't such a good idea after all. This is probably the reason we have not strung popcorn for the tree in years. I had forgotten. I think we will eat what is left of the good popcorn and throw out what is on the tree. There is no way we can go through this during the holidays. It is bad enough on Christmas Eve when the dog and cat hide the carrots for the reindeer, drink the milk, and eat the cookies for Santa! We always have to put everything out again before going to bed."

The doorbell rang and Midnight started barking. It was Pastor Johnstone. "Hi all!" he said as he patted Midnight on her head. "You forgot to take your holiday poinsettias from the church. You had ordered two in memory of your mother and Howard's father."

"Oh, thank you so much, Tom," I said, "and welcome to the nut house. I guess I am getting forgetful in my old age."

"Well, don't get too forgetful, because you are not that old," he said with a chuckle.

"Did I just see a string of popcorn go by followed by a dog in pursuit of a cat?" Tom asked.

"Yes; maybe they have their own tree! Anything is possible in this house," I said as I motioned for Tom to take a seat. "Would you like a cup of tea and some homemade cookies?"

"I will say no to the cup of tea, but I sure would like to try one of those delicious cookies to hold me over 'til dinner. I am on a mission, as my wife says," smiled Tom.

"How is Mildred?" I asked. "I did not get a chance to speak with her after church last Sunday."

"She is well; thank you. I will tell her you asked about her," replied Tom. "She really enjoyed spending the day shopping and having lunch with you and Lenora Lee a few weeks back."

"We did have a really nice day, and Lenora Lee is a wonderful person. I am glad she and her children settled here in our community," I said, smiling at Tom. As a change of subject, I added, "The church decorations are lovely. I am sure the angels in heaven heard the choir sing last Sunday."

"I am sure the angels heard one little girl sing," Tom said, and he smiled at Susan as her head popped up from gathering popcorn to listen to the conversation.

"She loves singing the Christmas songs. She is not shy," I said.

"Dress warm for the live nativity. The weatherman on Channel Eight News said we might have snow flurries, but I believe they are predicting some snow accumulation. Actually, it seems odd not to have some snow on the ground for Christmas Eve," Tom said. "I can't remember the last Christmas without snow on the ground."

"I am glad that the nativity is at five o'clock in the afternoon and the church service is at seven so that the children will not be out late on Christmas Eve. It is then that we put baby Jesus in our manger, and Howard, with one of the children's help, puts the star on the top of the tree. We light the Advent candle. Then the children put out the milk and cookies for Santa and the dog will eat them. Then we put our family gifts under the tree and wait for Midnight to sniff all the presents and Kit-Kat to pull off all the bows and ribbons. Andrew puts out carrots for the reindeer. The dog and cat hide them."

"Jeanette usually reads *The Visit of St. Nick*. Next, starting with my dad, we read the Christmas story from the Bible. We love the children to have the magic of Santa, but we insist they know and respect the Christ of Christmas."

"Then Howard's mother says a prayer and gives a little Christmas message. She is very good at composing poems and short stories. We are blessed by her prayers. If it is too late in the evening, she will wait and do all of this on Christmas Day, and then she'll just say a short prayer. Last is hanging the stockings, and then the children are off to bed. Amen!"

"Wow, your Christmas Eve is too busy for me. We have the live nativity and church and then relax and go to bed. You have a nice family. We are glad you are part of our church family," Tom said, and then he added, "Well, I must be going now; lots to do! Thank you for the delicious cookies," and he headed for the door.

"Thank you, Pastor Tom; we are happy attending church there, and thank you for delivering the poinsettias. See you in church—bye now!"

I shut the door quickly as soon as he was out on the porch. The air was very cold and there were snow flurries. The tree branches were bending from the force of the wintry wind.

CHAPTER 12

Today is December 23. This is the day when I look at my list to see if everything is done, is getting done, or is on schedule to be done. Kevin is in his bouncy seat and having the time of his life. He is feeling better now, and is laughing and giggling so loudly that I laugh as I watch him. I have to bake the pies today. Dad and Jeanette will be here late this afternoon. Howard's mom will spend tonight and tomorrow night with us, too. She could come tomorrow morning, but she enjoys spending time with my sister and father, and we have plenty of room and want her to be with us. Tomorrow we will eat finger foods and homemade chicken noodle soup. I checked my menu for Christmas dinner; turkey with all the trimmings. I proceeded to bake an apple and pumpkin pie. On Christmas day I will make real whipped cream too.

"Did you know Mr. Green will be alone this Christmas?" Howard stated.

"No," I said. "Why?"

Mr. and Mrs. Green welcomed us when we first moved here. They helped make the transition from one state to another more pleasant. She showed me the town and the best places to shop, and she brought us dinner and introduced us to the congregation of the Skippack United Methodist Church. They have two sons. One lives in Canada with his wife and family of five children. They visit occasionally. The other son lives in New Hampshire, not far away. He has three children: a boy and two girls. Mrs. Green passed away a little over two years ago. We miss her terribly, and we know how much Mr. Green still grieves for his wife.

Howard continued. "His son and grandson are in the hospital. His son had a hip replacement, and his grandson broke his leg playing football. His daughter-in-law will be catering to them and will not be able to come to take him to their house on Christmas Day. Do you think he would like to join us for Christmas dinner? I would like to invite him here. I don't want him to be alone on Christmas."

"That would be a great idea. Would you ask him, please?" I said.

"I think he and your dad would get along just fine. We can send food over to his son and family to make it easy on his daughter-in-law when her husband and son are released from the hospital. How does that sound to you, Kim?"

"Sounds like a plan to me," I said, smiling at my wonderful husband.

"Instead of calling him, I will stop by his house while I am out shopping," Howard said. "He may need a few things anyway, and I could do that for him."

"Shopping, are you?" I murmured as I winked at my husband.

"Oh, maybe just a few little items for the kids," Howard whispered.

"Uh-huh." I smiled. "Will you be near a Tiffany's?" I asked him.

"Of course; isn't that near Bailey, Banks, and Biddle, another expensive, lavish jewelry store?" he asked.

"I want only the best," I said. "Then again, I already have the best," I added as I kissed him good bye.

Susan is skipping through the house. I decided to put on the radio and listen to the station playing only Christmas music. I sang along to "Rockin' Around the Christmas Tree." The next song was the one Susan sang in school, so she was ready. She sang along and did all the hand motions she learned for her performance in the school program.

Up on the housetop reindeer pause,
Out jumps good old Santa Claus.
Down through the chimney with lots of toys,
All for the little ones, Christmas joys.

At this point, her arms go up and her hands go on her hips for the next lines:

Ho-ho-ho! Who wouldn't go?
Ho-ho-ho! Who wouldn't go?
Up on the housetop, click, click, click,
Down through the chimney with old St. Nick.

We were hugging, laughing, and singing—and making Christmas memories to last a lifetime. Kevin was in his highchair clapping his hands.

Today Howard does his holiday shopping. Well, it is not December 24, the day before Christmas, when he usually remembers to shop! However, it is the day before the day before, so he is early this year. I was lucky in late November to have Howard's mother watch Kevin so I could go shopping alone by myself one day, and she watched him another day so that I could meet my friends for lunch. I needed it. I enjoyed a girls' days out without children. How often does that happen?

Andrew and his friend are in the family room playing a Wii game. This game system was a great investment. It is enjoyable because there are so many different games to play. All of us play something from time to time, and it is a great way to be physically active indoors when it is too cold to play outside.

I like the bowling game because I win. Howard enjoys the downhill skiing game. I cannot do that, and I would seriously injure a lot of skiers if I tried! My friend Ann and I try to do the exercise games as long as Howard isn't home to make comments, such as, "She said touch your toes, not your knees!" or "You grew it, now you lift it!" Usually one of us throws a pillow at him.

"Andrew, did you clean your room and get your gifts wrapped?" I asked.

"I will, mom," he said.

"Well, I think it is time to say goodbye to your friends and get things done. Your aunt, your grandfather, and your grandmother will be here this afternoon," I said. "Tomorrow is Christmas Eve, so let's get things done now."

Suddenly, I saw a bright red flash. The flash looked like Katie moving rather rapidly across the room. I called, "Katie, could you come here please?"

"Oh, Mom, I am really busy getting ready to go out, and I have to dry my hair and get dressed."

"Well, I want to see you before you leave," I commented. "Who is taking you where?"

"Annie's mother is driving us to the mall. Remember you said I could go," Katie yelled back.

"I do not want you out all day. Your grandparents and aunt will be here later, and I would like you to be here when they arrive," I said. "Are you coloring your hair?"

"I just changed it a little bit, Mom."

"When you are finished, I want to see you."

About fifteen minutes later, I heard Andrew wailing in laughter and yelling, "You are in trouble—you are in trouble!"

In trouble? I did not like the sound of that word. I heard her in the hall closet getting a coat, so I called to her and told her again to come and see me. I was starting to get angry with her. Katie peeked around the corner of the dining room. The next thing I knew this bright red head was in front of me.

"Oh my goodness—it's red! What have you done to your hair? Is this just for Christmas, or is it a belated Halloween gag? Your father is not going to be happy."

"Oh, Mom, how do you like it? I love it. Isn't it wild?"

"Yes, wild, that is a good word for it. It is wild! Oh Katie, how could you change your hair color now without saying something to me first. Maybe if you went to an auburn or strawberry blonde color, it wouldn't be so shocking, but this? You look like a deranged rooster! Oh, Katie, it is just awful. Your father is going to have a fit," I scolded. "I am going to have a fit!"

"Oh, Mom, relax, it's not that bad. Do you think that after Christmas I could get it cut, styled, and spiked just a little? It will look cute, and then you won't mind the color So much."

Still furious and in a state of disbelief, I said, "Katie, I mind the color! Since you are going out today anyway, you are stopping at the Market-Basket supermarket and buying a color close to your own hair. Then I want you to return home and re-color that hair instead of going out with the girls. Your friends can wait until after Christmas. You should talk with me before you do something like this. Spike your hair—I don't think so!"

"But, Mom, I told my friends how cool you are, and that you wouldn't mind."

"Well, you told your friends wrong," I said. "Katie, God knows I love you dearly. You were our first-born child. You are my daughter, and I am your mother, and you will only go with the girls to get another hair color and come home and redo your hair. You are not going to the mall. Do you understand me?"

"But, Mom..."

"And another thing—I used to be a cool mom, but right now I am pretty hot, as in angry! Your aunt, your grandfather, and your grandmother will be here soon. What were you thinking?"

I was livid. I saw the tears and the anger, but she knew I was angry, too, and she was wrong in not discussing this with me first. She is only fourteen.

Out she stormed with her friends. A short time later, she returned and showed me a hair color very close to her own beautiful dark hair. "Thank you," I said, and I smiled to show her that I was no longer angry. "Now go fix that head before your father sees it. You are already in trouble, because I am sure Andrew told your father. Don't come downstairs until it looks nice." She stomped upstairs without a word.

"Children—no wonder parents go insane; we inherit it from our kids!"

I know we have five senses—seeing, hearing, smelling, feeling, and tasting—but I think there should be another one: common sense!

The phone rang. It was Margaret's brother, Howard's uncle Edward and his wife, Judy, calling to see if they could come over this evening to visit with my father and sister.

"Oh, that would be very nice," I said. "They should be here soon. How about visiting between seven or seven-thirty?" I asked. "I baked a couple of pies. Oh great; see you then." I wasn't worried if the pies I'd intended for Christmas dinner got eaten tonight. I could always make other desserts for Christmas day.

Just then, we could hear the fire truck moving along our street. Santa and Mrs. Claus were tossing candy to all the neighborhood children. Andrew, Susan, and their playmates ran out onto the porch to wave at Santa and collect the candy. Suddenly, in unison, Andrew and Susan were yelling that carolers were on the front lawn singing. When I was a teenager, we would go caroling from street to street and house to house in the frigid cold and then back to the church for hot cocoa. It was fun and rewarding, especially for the senior adults and shut-ins who would smile with delight and sing along with us. Spreading the Christmas message in song is a fun way to meet and greet folks during the holidays.

The kids came back inside and began playing question and answer games.

"Where is the Kentucky Derby?"

"Kentucky, stupid!"

"Who is buried in Grant's tomb?"

"Mickey Mouse, you moron!"

"If you have six fingers on one hand, how many would you have on the other?"

I'd had all I could take. "Ok, Susan and Andrew, it is time for your friends to go home now," I said. "Our company will be here soon. Merry Christmas, kids, but everyone has to go home now. I told you both before. Now say good-bye and go wrap gifts or clean; do whatever needs to be done so you won't have it to do when your aunt and grandparents are here. You children are all starting to push my wrong buttons, and I am getting angry. Now go do what you were told to do. I am glad you enjoyed the time with your friends, but we are having company soon, so say goodbye."

I made the soup for tomorrow. When I looked out the window, I saw my sister's car pull into the driveway. I went out to greet her and Dad. "Hi, you both look wonderful. Here come Susan and Andrew. Look at you, Sis, a brand new car; wow! You work hard and deserve it."

"I just love it, Kim. It is a Honda Accord. What do you think of this color? It is called champagne. I will take you for a spin later." Jeanette was elated. "Andrew, look how big you are growing, and Susan, I want to hear your songs."

"Hi, Grandpa, we love you!"

"Ha, bribery will get you nowhere!" Dad shouted back at them. "It is so much colder here than at home. Where's that little Kevin? I cannot wait to see him."

I laughed and said, "He should be awake from his nap any minute now, Dad."

"Where's Katie?" asked Jeanette.

"Oh, she will be along shortly," I answered. "Uncle Ed and Aunt Judy just called. They will be here this evening to visit."

"It will be good to see them. It has been awhile since we saw them last," Dad said.

Jeanette and I would spend the afternoon and evening catching up on family news and enjoying the closeness that only sisters share. That would give Dad and Howard's mom time to be with their grandchildren. Minutes after I had greeted my dad and sister, I could see Margaret's car coming down the street. As she pulled into the driveway, she rolled down her window and said, "How is this for perfect timing? We almost pulled in at the same time."

I laughed and said, "Hi, Mom. Did you two plan that?"

"No," said Mom, "but I can't wait to take a spin in that pretty new car. I love the color; it's almost like a blend of gold and silver."

Jeanette smiled and said, "They call it champagne. After dinner we will go for a spin. Aunt Judy can come with us, too."

It was fun to get together with my family members to talk and reminisce. Uncle Edward is a bit quieter than Margaret is. Then again, everyone is quieter than Margaret is. She mentioned how she told the children about when Ed and she were little and went to Philadelphia for Christmas shopping with their mother.

"Oh, yes, I remember how we would look forward to that day every year. Then we would come home and tell Dad at dinner about our day and show him our presents. He would always ask us what we had asked Santa Claus to bring us," Edward said.

"Aunt Judy, are you still writing poetry?" Jeanette asked. "I remember you had just written a book of poetry last time we saw you."

"Oh yes, some, but not as much at this time," Judy answered. "You do know the book was published? It is small, but I like it. A person has to start somewhere with her writings."

"That's wonderful," said Jeanette. "What is the book called, and where can we purchase it?"

"You, Margaret, and Kim do not have to purchase it, because I brought each of you one for Christmas," Judy said, as she passed them to us.

We each said thank you. The little book of poetry was titled *Poetry by Judy.*

"Oh, this is lovely, Aunt Judy, thank you," I said. "I remember you mentioning last year that you were seriously thinking of writing a book using the religious poems you had written. My mother's friend in New Jersey wrote a little book this year. It was published in November. Her book is titled *One Lucky Pound Puppy*. It is her first book, too. It is a true story of the puppy she and her husband adopted from a local animal shelter."

Changing the subject, I asked, "Uncle Ed and Aunt Judy, would you like to join us for breakfast tomorrow at about nine o'clock? The nine of us always have a big breakfast on Christmas Eve morning."

"Oh, that would be so nice. Is that ok with you, Ed?" Judy asked her husband.

"Sounds good to me; what can we bring?" asked Ed.

"How about some Danish and cinnamon buns," I said.

"Alright, we have it covered," Ed replied. "See you in the morning. Goodnight, all!"

On Christmas Eve morning, we have a real country breakfast with the help of my sister and Howard's mom. We start with muffins—blueberry, pumpkin, and banana—and then we make eggs, bacon, sausage, pancakes, orange juice, fruit, and coffee. It is wonderful to have the family together.

While we were eating breakfast, the phone rang and it was Benjamin Green. He was accepting our invitation for Christmas dinner. I always wrap an extra gift for a man, woman, or child in case someone pops in unexpectedly. That way they do not have to sit and watch everyone else open presents and have nothing of their own to open. I decided to call Howard and ask him to pick out another gift for Mr. Green while he is out shopping for me. He will then have two gifts to open.

Christmas Eve, late at night, is a special time, a quiet time, just for me. How can that be with all these other people around? It is usually very late after everyone has gone to bed. I love to sit with just the Christmas tree lights on and meditate on this day and my life: the past, the present, and looking to the future (and sometimes that is only as far as Christmas Eve and Christmas Day). A calming sense of peace comes over me as I think of Mary, a very young woman, pregnant and riding on a donkey as she ponders the magnitude of soon giving birth to the Son of God. I think of a man having to deliver a baby—a very special baby—in a stable of all places. I think of how they must place their newborn Son in a trough, a manger with straw, surrounded by animals. There were animal smells, animal waste, and animal noises around them. They would not have the cleanliness or comfort of a room in an inn. One would not think a king would be born in a stable. Mary was so young, but God believed in her love and faithfulness to carry our Savior and care for him. Mary was "highly favored" by God.

Our God is an awesome God!

CHAPTER 13

We all slept a little later today; it was Christmas Eve, and quite cold, but the sun was shining and it was just beautiful. My sister, Howard's mom, and I are preparing our Christmas Eve breakfast.

"How about after breakfast I take you and Margaret for a ride in my new car?" Jeanette asked.

"Oh, that would be great; we never did get a chance to do that last night because of the company," I answered.

"Hi, Grand-mom and Aunt Jeanette," we heard Andrew and Susan say as they greeted Margaret and Jeanette in the kitchen.

"Merry Christmas Eve, everybody," said Margaret as she kissed everyone. "I know we have muffins, but I also made this cinnamon coffee cake that I know your father likes."

Margaret is a character and a lot of fun. She was wearing a holiday sweater and Christmas jewelry. To top off her outfit, she had on an elf hat and slipper-type shoes that curled up at the toes with bells on the ends. I would call them elf shoes.

"Whoa," laughed Katie as she came into the dining room. "Look at you, Grand-mom; the fashion police will be all over you. You look like an elf."

Katie had her long hair pulled back into a ponytail. She looked cute, and more like the daughter I knew now that her hair was back to her normal color.

"Your hair looks nice, Katie," I said.

She rolled her eyes. She knew what I was referring to, but she said, "Thanks, Mom."

"Oh, Mom, that was so nice of you to make this coffee cake," I commented. "We have so many good things to eat. Could you call everyone for breakfast? Uncle Edward and Aunt Judy should be here soon."

"Oh, of course," said Margaret. "Come and get it!" she screamed as she scooped up Kevin in her arms. We all laughed. *I could have done that*, I thought to myself.

Dad came downstairs and into the kitchen. "I see Santa's helpers have arrived," he said as he looked at Margaret.

"Oh, come here you old man and give me a hug," she said as she laughed. The funny thing is they are the same age. I am so glad that everyone gets along. Oh, there have been some disagreements in the past, but praise the Lord, they have been nothing that we couldn't put behind us and go on as a loving family.

"Muffins and cinnamon cake, all right!" yelled Andrew.

"Did I hear cinnamon cake? You know I want some of that," said Dad.

"Here come Uncle Ed and Aunt Judy," yelled Andrew.

"Howard, did you get a couple of extra chairs for the table?" I asked.

"No, but I will right now," answered Howard.

"Merry Christmas Eve, everyone," Ed and Judy said as they came through the door.

"The weatherman now says we will have more than just snow flurries tonight; it is actually going to snow. It sure is cold. It is that damp cold that goes right through you," remarked Ed.

"We went to the European bakery in town for the Danishes and cinnamon buns. Everything in that place looks so delicious, you just want to taste it all," commented Judy.

I laughed, "Oh yes, it all is wonderful until you have to pay for it and get fat. We love it, too, but we try not to venture in there very often. Just to walk through the door is heavenly, smelling the baked goods and breads."

Kevin was eating blueberries off his highchair tray. He was beginning to look like one big berry. He had blue stains in his hair, on his face, and everywhere else. He seemed to like them, though, and was enjoying himself, and they were keeping him occupied. Midnight always stays really close to him when he is in the highchair, hoping for a handout. Kit-Kat stopped eating his food and came over to bat the blueberries around the room.

"There goes one, Mom, right under the refrigerator!" laughed Katie.

Christmas movies are on the television. I just love them. Of course, every year Howard teases me, "Each and every year you watch these same movies over and over again. I know you know the songs, but you must know the dialogue by now, too."

"But, Howard, these are wonderful movies, and maybe they put a tear in your eye or a smile on your face, but usually they touch your heart."

"There is so much violence, sex, and obscene language in television programs these days. However, during the Christmas season, movies such as *White Christmas*, my favorite, are about doing something wonderful for someone else. They are uplifting, family movies. They are lighthearted, and the songs are wonderful. Sometimes they are a bit of a fantasy, but so are the superhero films, and we watch them, too," I said.

As though she had read my mind, Margaret started singing, "When you're worried and you can't sleep, just count your blessings instead of sheep." This song is from the movie *White Christmas*.

Howard walked over and kissed me. "Kim, I love you. How did God pick a special woman like you to be my wife and the mother of my children?"

I answered, "He must have seen me searching for you." I put my arms around Howard and gave him a big hug.

Howard went outside to figure out why some of the Christmas lights were not on. I have confidence in him. God bless him, because it is so cold.

"Look, Mommy, see the reindeer on my shirt? And I have reindeer on my socks, too!" shouted Susan.

"Wow, look at you! Do you know what day this is?"

"Santa Claus comes tonight!" she screamed. She screamed so loudly I believe the dishes rattled.

"Yes, and tomorrow you can wear the pretty red dress Aunt Jeanette bought for you," I said. "What am I thinking? You can wear the dress tonight when we go to church." I turned to my family and said, "Wait until you all see Andrew dressed in his sport coat; wow!" I smiled.

I love when we are all together as a family. I believe going to church, family prayer, togetherness, and real involvement in each other's lives has kept us close. I know families in which people ignore each other and literally hurt each other. I don't understand it; life is too short to argue over petty things. It is good to talk through a problem and know why each person feels the way he or she does. Both sides need to come to a resolution. That way, no one is clueless as to why a person may be acting the way he or she is. Treating another person cruelly is not acceptable.

Nothing is worse than knowing there is a problem and not identifying it. Really caring about another person's feelings and being honest means everything in a relationship. We are a family and want the best for one another. I am so thankful that we care for and love each other. We do not always agree on everything. We are all different human beings. I like chocolate and Howard likes vanilla. I tell him vanilla is boring. Not always agreeing is human; it is not bad. God created each one of us unique and special. Of course, I do jokingly tell Howard I am always right! God bless our family and friends.

Love is patient, love is kind. It does not envy, it does not boast, it is not proud. It is not rude, it is not self-seeking, it is not easily angered, it keeps no record of wrongs. Love does not delight in evil but rejoices with the truth. It always protects, always trusts, always hopes, always perseveres.

1 Corinthians: 13:4-7 (NIV)

Love never fails. And now these three remain:
Faith, hope, and love.
But the greatest of these is love.

1 Corinthians 13:13 (NIV)

Susan is now singing "Jingle Bells." She is always singing something, and it fills our house with joy.

"What are you going to do after Christmas when you won't be singing Christmas songs anymore?" Howard asked her.

"I don't know; maybe I will sing Easter songs," she said. I believe Howard felt defeated.

The sky is darkening as the snow clouds approach. "We are having snow tonight," Howard whispered. If the kids heard the word *snow*, they would get even more excited.

Snow on Christmas Eve—yes, that is what we all would like. "Hey, if it snows on Christmas, maybe we could all go for a sleigh ride the day after Christmas," said Howard.

"Oh, that would be so much fun." I turned to Dad and Jeanette and said, "I know you want to leave early to return home, but you can stay the morning I hope; please?"

Jeanette looked at Dad, and he nodded yes.

"Yes, let's do a sleigh ride!" Jeanette shouted. "But right now, let's go for a ride in my new car," she said. Mom and I grabbed our coats, and the three of us headed out and climbed into Jeanette's car.

"It has that new car smell," said Margaret. "It is just like bringing home a new baby or puppy; always that wonderful new scent."

I laughed. "This car is so nice, Sis. I really love it. I wish you good luck with it, too. So while I have you away from Daddy, tell me, how has he been, really? You know there could be something wrong, and he would never tell me."

"Kim, he is doing really well," Jeanette said. "You know I would tell you otherwise."

"Ok," I said.

"Oh, my Greek friend says that you should always drop money, change that is, on the floor of a new car for good luck," I said.

"Really? I never heard that," commented Jeanette.

"Well, guess what, girls?" Margaret said. "If I get a new car, I do not want to see or hear any change on the floor. I want to feel and hear the swishing of paper money falling on my floor."

We laughed at her. "What year is your car, Margaret?" Jeanette asked. "It is getting pretty old now?"

"It is a 2005," Margaret said. "Yes, one of these days I will have to look for another one, I suppose, but it still runs great."

"This is a Honda Accord, but the Honda Civic is a nice little car, too," remarked Jeanette. "It would be less expensive to buy and great for you to zip around in with your friends. I don't think you drive that far anymore, do you?"

"Oh, I do sometimes," answered Margaret. "Don't tie me down yet. The Civic looks like a nice little car, but I am not sure what I want to get. Howard says I should look now before the end of the year in order to get a better deal. Who knows what I may be driving next time I see you!"

Jeanette laughed and said, "Nothing would surprise me."

"One thing is for sure, you will not see me on a motorcycle," Margaret said. "Those things scare me to death on the highway, and if possible, I try to stay away from them. They drive too fast, and the people are not protected very well. I know they have the shield in front, but I do not want to be picking bugs out of my teeth. I don't want the wind in my face or to be splashed with mud, and I want a roof over my head, air conditioning, and heat. Besides, I want four wheels under me, not two, and where would I put everything when I go shopping?"

"I could see you on a motorcycle," Jeanette said, and she laughed.

CHAPTER 14

Skippack looks so beautiful during the holidays. Even with no snow on the ground and just snow flurries, the decorations, the lights, and even the people are joyous. Sometimes we just jump into the car and ride around the community to look at the lovely decorations and lights. The store windows have animated figures in them, and are trimmed in mistletoe and holly. The light posts have wreaths, and Christmas lights are across the main street in town. The church bells ring from the Skippack United Methodist Church, and three times a day a short medley of Christmas hymns play.

It seems we are all preparing for Christmas Eve or Christmas Day except for the cat and dog. They are quite content resting in front of the fireplace. Dad went to take a nap, as did Kevin, so they will be rested and awake for tonight's live nativity and church service. Margaret commented that a television movie was coming on soon that she wanted to watch, so she was off to the family room. "I bet she falls asleep in there," I whispered to Jeanette. Jeanette nodded in agreement. Jeanette and I are preparing everything we can for tomorrow.

"We need to decide on desserts. I used the pies last night for our company," I said. "How about I bake a holiday gift cake and a German chocolate cake?" I asked. "The gift cake is the one made with cream cheese, cherries, and nuts."

"Well, you make the one and I will make the other," said Jeanette.

I am glad my sister is here. I have missed her terribly. Even though we live far from one another and there are years between us in age, we have always been close at heart. She is my confidant, my other half, my partner in crime, my strength when needed, and always my best friend.

Unless you are a sister who has a sister, you
cannot really know the depth of a sister's love.

When any problem, fear, happiness, or worry troubles me, I just pick up the phone and call Jeannette. She is always at the other end cheering me on, calming my fears, solving my problems, or just telling me she loves me. We talk and pray together, and everything is all right.

Thank you, God, for sisters.
Sisters are different flowers from the same garden.

"Guess what?" Margaret said as she walked into the kitchen. "I forgot all the presents! I left them in bags by the door to carry and put them in the trunk. I can't believe I forgot them!" We laughed, remembering past Christmases when she had done the same thing.

"Mom, you are too funny! Hey, Sis, remember when our family dog, Fluffy, tried to eat all the popcorn and gingerbread men from the tree? That tree was a mess! Or when we had freezing rain and no one went to church because the mayor wanted all unnecessary vehicles off the streets; that was the year we were to transport people to church and could not. Remember the time we put the turkey in the oven and set it to 450 degrees instead of 350 degrees? We went out to the porch to decorate the windows, and when we came back in, we saw smoke billowing out of the kitchen. Needless to say, the turkey was more than well done that year!"

We all laughed, and I continued. "Mother did not get angry; she simply said, 'Well, everyone, we will have ham,' and she proceeded to open a canned ham. She was the best, and so was our Christmas dinner!"

We had a wonderful mother. As the saying goes, if life handed her lemons, she made lemonade. Well almost—knowing our mother, she would make lemon meringue pie! Our mother had a little tradition each year at Christmas; she would give my sister and me a calendar towel, a box of chocolate-covered cherries, and a poinsettia. Now that we are older, we really miss our mother and that tradition. At Easter, she would give each of us a beautiful hyacinth.

I always tell the children and Howard that we have to show and tell the people near us that we love them. Do n't be afraid to give a smile or a hug. That just may be what the person needs today. Do not be too fast in judging other folks. They may just be having a bad day. We should be like Susan, who always says, "Mommy, if they do not have a smile, I will give them one of mine."

One day on the television, I watched the television show Britain's Got Talent. A woman sang the song "I Dreamed a Dream" from the musical Les Miserables. When asked what was her dream, she answered she wanted to sing professionally. She knew she has a wonderful voice and could sing. She made the comment that she had never been given the chance to perform in front of an audience. I give her credit. After seeing her competition, she was brave to walk out on to that stage. She was mocked, because she was older, or because she was just not as young or sexy as some of the other contestants. Because of that, the judges and audience members assumed she had no talent. They rolled their eyes and were judging her before they heard her sing.

Did she prove them wrong! The audience was breathless when she opened her mouth to sing. She received a standing ovation. She sang beautifully and captured the hearts of everyone. All she needed was that chance. We need to give everyone a chance. We may not know what trials that another person is going through. I love to hear her sing this song. Her voice is beautiful.

Never judge a book by its cover
Think of an M & M candy when you are ready to judge another----
The outside is just a shell covering, but the good chocolate candy is inside
With a person maybe his or her shell is rough, but Inside God looks at the heart.

Back to the topic of Margaret's memory lapse, I said, "Oh, Mom, it is so funny for you to have left the gifts, because we were just talking about all the crazy things that used to happen in our family at Christmas time when Jeannette and I were girls. Andrew is at his friend's house, but he will come home soon, and you can take him with you to get everything and bring it back by dinner time, ok?"

Margaret decided not to wait for Andrew to come home, and she set off to get him from his friend's house down the street. She has a heart of gold, and sometimes she really makes us laugh. Sometimes she wraps gifts but forgets which gift is which, and when we open them, they are for another person. I have seen her go out with two different shoes on and not realize it. We love her and she keeps life interesting and amusing. She has answered the phone only for the doorbell to ring, at which point she tells the caller to hold a moment while she gets the door, and then she forgets that someone is on the phone waiting for her to return to the call.

One of the funniest times was shopping with her in a department store. I was looking at handbags and she had gone to the ladies' room. When I looked up to see Margaret walking toward me, I saw a trail of toilet tissue dragging on the floor behind her as she walked through the store. I could not stop laughing. I went over to her as quickly as possible to step on it and anchor it down so that she could dislodge it from her shoes and we could throw it away. All we could do was stand there and laugh.

I said to her, "I couldn't get to you fast enough."

She commented with a wink, "I am saving it for later."

"Will you get stopped for shoplifting?" I teased.

We were hysterical with laughter.

One day we went to the mall. We parked near JC Penney. It was Margaret, Kevin, and me, as the other children were in school. We went in different directions and said we would meet at three o'clock at the same place—at the entrance to JC Penney.

The time was almost three o'clock when my cell phone rang.

"Kim, oh my, the car has been stolen!" yelled Margaret. "I am here in the parking lot outside of JC Penney and I cannot find your car. Oh Kim, I am so upset."

I could hear the panic in her voice. "Ok, Mom, calm down; I am coming out the door now. Just stay there and we will call the police," I told her. I walked outside and there was my car where I had parked it. But, where was Mom? Then it dawned on me; she had gone out a different door. I telephoned her back.

"Mom, I think you went out the wrong door. We parked outside the shoe department. What door did you take to exit the store?" I asked.

"I don't know," she answered. Let me walk into the store. I am in the jewelry department," she said after a few moments.

"Mom, you went out the wrong door!" I said.

All I could hear was her cheerful laughter and a man's voice asking, "Lady, did you find your car yet?"

Margaret keeps us jumping, but we love her for it.

I have learned that like the weather, I cannot control or change her. The weather will be what it will be, and I have to adjust to it. My father always says that neither time nor tide waits for anyone. Our attitude is 99 percent of how we react to situations. Starting with a good attitude always helps. It is so much easier to smile than frown. I would rather like someone and hope they will like me, too, than be unkind to anyone. Rumors and gossip are on the tongue of the devil. It is so easy to gossip, and sometimes it is hard to keep our mouths shut. I try to tell myself to listen more and talk less. I know Howard would like that, but who is asking Howard?

Everyone was busy getting ready for the holiday. Katie was wrapping and cleaning, Howard was out running errands, and Susan was cleaning her room, or at least that is what I thought.

Another Christmas is upon us. Think of the brightest star shining in the night sky leading the wise men. Think of heavenly singing and angels proclaiming a baby's birth—not just any baby, but Christ the King, our Savior.

Alleluia!

The doorbell rang and I saw Howard's mother standing there with Andrew, both with arms full of presents. "Hi, Mom, back again so soon?" I teased. "Merry Christmas! This is perfect timing, because dinner is ready. I see you dressed appropriately for this cold evening. Let me take your coat. I can feel the cold when I open this door. It is really going to be cold tonight. Thank you, Andrew for helping your Grand-mom."

Howard's mother always looks lovely, whether she is at home cleaning or going out for the day. She is from the "old school," and believes a woman should always wear makeup, jewelry, and nice clothes. She looked tailored in her skirt and jacket. She had on shoe boots, a long woolen coat, a scarf, gloves, and a hat, which she peeled off when she stepped into the warmth of the house.

"Where is my littlest sweetheart, Kevin?" she asked.

"Oh, Dad or Jeanette, or maybe even Susan, will be bringing him downstairs soon," I said.

Andrew was carrying in the bags with the gifts. Margaret threw her arms around him and said, "Thanks again, Andrew; you were a big help. The gifts are here on time."

"Dinner is ready," I called. "We want to eat early so we can change our clothes for church and the live nativity. Then hopefully we can get to church on time."

Last year Howard was one of the shepherds and Katie played Mary. She was so young, only thirteen, but we were proud of her. It made us stop and realize just how young Mary was when she gave birth to Jesus.

Katie had finished setting the table, and Jeanette was placing dinner on the table. Mom was filling the glasses with beverages. I saw Dad coming down the stairs. "Katie, call your father for dinner. I believe he is in the garage."

Dad said, "I guess little Kevin is with his father. He wasn't in his crib so I figured he was changed and already down here for dinner."

"No, he is not with Howard; he is coming through the back door now with Andrew."

"Where's Susan?" Dad questioned. "I have not seen her since I lay down to take my nap." I started calling for her as I neared the bottom of the stairs.

"Susan, come on, dinner is ready now." No answer; so again I called with no answer.

Howard reminded us again that we would have to dress warmly tonight. "It is that type of cold night that chills to the bone."

I asked, "Howard, have you seen Susan?"

"No, I thought she was cleaning her room."

"I thought so, too. Even Kevin has not awakened from his nap. Dad, you said Kevin was not in his crib?"

"He wasn't there before I came downstairs, and I did not see or hear little Susan either," Dad said.

I ran up the stairs and looked in Susan's room, which was nice and clean. Seeing no one there, I went to our room, but again, not a sign of either of them. I tried to stay calm since I did not believe they would leave the house or someone would come in and take them, but the fact remained that my two youngest children were gone.

For any parent that this has happened to, a chill and an immediate fear takes over your whole body. I ran back downstairs and said to Howard, "My God, where are my little girl and baby boy?" Howard could see I was beginning to panic; I was shaking and about to cry. He put his arms around me to comfort me.

"She can't be far," he said.

"Far? She should not have left the house, and with the baby!"

"Maybe she took Kevin for a walk," chimed in Katie.

"In this weather? On Christmas Eve? All alone and knowing we are going to eat early and go to the nativity and church service?"

Suddenly, Andrew ran out of the room, and within what seemed like only seconds, he returned and announced that the baby's stroller was gone, so Susan must have taken Kevin for a walk.

"A walk?" I screeched. "She did not ask permission to go anywhere, especially not with her baby brother on Christmas Eve. It is starting to snow! I don't know whether to cry or scream!"

"Should we call the police?" asked Jeanette.

"I cannot believe she would do something like this. I know the children have had their friends in and out the last couple of days, but none of us saw her take Kevin out," I remarked, still shaking.

"I am sorry, honey, but I was asleep with the bedroom door shut," said Dad, feeling guilty for the fact that he had not seen them.

"Oh, Dad, it is not your fault. I just want to know where my children are."

Howard picked up the phone and said, "I am calling Officer Jim McCall. He is a good guy, and hopefully he will be able to assist us in some way. We do not know how Susan and Kevin are dressed. She knows better than to pull a stunt like this."

"And it is Christmas Eve," I whispered.

"Hi, could I speak with Officer McCall? This is Howard Turner from Deerwood Drive." Howard paused for a moment while he waited. "Hi, Jim, this is Howard Turner. I know this will sound crazy, but our youngest daughter and son are both missing."

"What?" Jim shouted.

"I don't think it is foul play, or at least we pray not. We think Susan, our six-year-old daughter, took her ten-month-old baby brother out for a walk. His name is Kevin."

"Maybe they went to see the Christmas lights," I murmured. I could barely speak. "Could you please put it on speaker phone?" I asked.

Howard hit the speakerphone button and said, "We think she is pushing him in his stroller."

"Ok, I will head out now. It will be dark soon. I will tell the other officers to keep an eye out for a little girl and a baby boy. Do you remember what they are wearing?"

I replied, "No, she left from her room when everyone was busy and no one saw her leave. She has strawberry blonde hair, and it is long. Wait, I do remember; she showed me her reindeer socks and shirt. She might have changed into her new red Christmas dress, though."

"Do you know anywhere she would go by herself?" asked Jim.

Howard chuckled and said, "Who knows? She is too independent for a six-year-old."

I could see the fear and questions on both Dad and Jeanette's faces. I remarked, "How did none of us see her take Kevin and his stroller out of the house? How did we not hear them?"

Katie said, "Mom, the stroller was in the mudroom, so she probably went out the side door while Granddad was asleep, and you and Aunt Jeanette were cooking. I was cleaning, but once I had done my side of the room, I vacuumed the other rooms. I was listening to music on my iPod, so I would not have heard her. Grand-mom was out with Andrew."

I headed to the family room coat closet. Suddenly, something made me stop with a jolt. I saw the manger with the shepherds, angel, and baby Jesus in place. "Oh, my goodness, I think I know where she is. Howard, come with me," I shouted.

"I'll drive," Howard said as he grabbed his coat and keys.

"We will be here if she comes home before you return," Jeanette said.

Howard's mom said, "Don't worry, Kim; I will say a prayer, and I know in my heart that Susie and Kevin are just fine. I will stay by the phone."

"Mom, how do you know where she is?" Katie asked. I did not answer her then, but said I would explain later, and Howard and I quickly jumped into the car.

"Where are we going?" asked Howard.

"Drive to the nativity. I believe that is where they are right now."

"Do you think she went by herself? Why wouldn't she wait to go with us this evening?" Howard asked.

"I don't know, but she knows we were all planning to go there before church. Let's just hope I am right."

"I noticed that the baby Jesus was in the manger at home. She had to be the one to put the figurine in there. Last night we were singing, 'Come to the Manger'."

It had started to snow, and the wind was blowing harder. There were quite a few people at the live nativity. We parked the car, and as we approached the manger, Howard's cell phone rang. At that same moment, we saw our young daughter; thank goodness she was wearing her coat and hat. She was sitting next to her brother and singing "Away in a Manger."

We saw Officer McCall walking toward us. "I was just calling to inform you that both of your little ones are here and safe," he said. I could see that Susan had wrapped Kevin's crib blanket around him to keep him warm, and his big eyes shone brightly under the hat of his snowsuit.

"She has Kevin sitting in the manger," Howard said.

"It doesn't seem like Susan to not ask us first before doing something like this," Howard said.

As we neared Susan and Kevin, we said, "There you are! You scared us half to death, young lady!"

"Oh, Mommy, Daddy, look, I did this all by myself. See, I put Kevin's snowsuit on and changed his diaper, too. I know he is warm under his bank-ket. He doesn't have any wad-dling clothes like baby Jesus, but he is warm and happy. I took the doll out and put Kevin in the manger. He did not cry, Mommy. My hands are cold. I forgot my mittens."

Howard and I looked at each other. Moments before, we had both wanted to scream, but after taking one look at our precious children, we were so happy just to find them safe. We both had tears in our eyes.

"Mommy, Daddy, I put the baby Jesus in our manger. It is Christmas Eve, you know."

We could hear Officer McCall clear his throat and chuckle. "Well, at least they are ok," he said.

"Thank you, Jim," we both said. "See you at church, or will it be too late?"

"It is never too late for church," he said. "Merry Christmas."

"Merry Christmas, Jim."

Howard asked, "Where is the stroller?"

"Oh, I hid it behind the manger. I put the doll in the stroller. I don't think Jesus had a stroller, did he, Mommy? And when Jesus grew up he had long hair like a girl!"

Howard spoke first. “Yes, we saw the baby Jesus in the manger at home. That was a nice thing to remember to do, as it is Christmas Eve; however, that still does not give you permission to take Kevin and come here without telling us. You knew we were coming to the nativity later as a family before church service. You should never leave the house without asking an adult. You have never done anything like this before, Susan. You know you have to ask permission first. You just do not leave without asking anyone. Now, let’s see your hands. They are cold and sore because you forgot your mittens.”

“Why is your brother in the manger?” I asked.

“I wanted to surprise you. Why have a doll when you can have a real baby boy!”

“The doll would have been fine,” I said.

Howard commented, “It is starting to snow more heavily now.”

Suddenly, Officer McCall, who had not left yet, walked up to Susan. Overhearing our conversation, he said, “I think I can handle this. Susan, if you go off again either by yourself or with your baby brother without asking your mommy or daddy’s permission first, I will have to arrest you and put you in jail.”

“Not on Christmas Eve!” howled Susan.

“Oh, yes, anytime you disobey or do something wrong. Your parents were worried and called the police to find you. I would like to be home with my family on Christmas Eve, too, but I had to look for you first. I am going home now, because I miss my little girl and boy.”

Susan’s face dropped. “I’m sorry, Mr. Policeman.” You could see the fear on her face and the tears in her eyes. “I just wanted to come to the manger and pretend Kevin was baby Jesus."

"Susan, you cannot leave the house just because you want to! You must always ask your father or me, and even then, we would never let you leave alone. I cannot believe you did that! Also, no one can ever take the place of Jesus. There was a doll in there and that is what should be there. You could have kept Kevin in his stroller. It is cold and snowing, and the wind is getting stronger now, too," I said.

"But everyone was asleep or busy."

"No, that is a bad answer and not a good excuse. I am never so busy that I cannot give you a yes or a no answer. You know you should be punished for this. I am angry now. You do know what you did was wrong, don't you? You did not ask me because you knew I would have said no to you bringing your baby brother here alone. Your father and I are very angry and upset with you." My voice grew louder.

"Yes, Mommy, I will ask first from now on," Susan whispered softly.

"I am sorry, Susan, but you must be punished," said Howard.

"But it is Christmas Eve, Daddy," she said.

"I do not care what day it is; you disobeyed. We will discuss it later," Howard said.

"We were worried about you and wanted you both to be safe. You see how it is snowing more now, and it is getting dark," Howard said. "I think the family will miss church service tonight. We are all cold and hungry, and Kevin is getting cranky, too. Besides, it is Christmas Eve, and we can go home and stay warm by the fire. We can hang the star on the tree and hang all the stockings. I know people in church will miss us, but I think it is better now just to go home. Is there anything we have forgotten to do?"

"Put milk and cookies out for Santa and carrots for the reindeer!" shouted Susan.

I joined in by saying, "We can read the story of Christmas and then off to bed to have sweet dreams tonight."

We drove slowly. We had some snow on the ground and the roads were becoming quite slippery. The weather forecast predicted eight to ten inches of snow for Christmas morning.

"So we are having a white Christmas after all," I commented as Howard started to sing along to "White Christmas," which was playing on the radio. I chimed in, singing, "And may all your Christmases be white."

CHAPTER 15

When Susan ran through the door, Dad, Howard's mom, my sister, Katie, and Andrew all asked where she had been.

"We have decided to miss the live nativity and church service this evening," Howard announced. "It is very cold and windy, and with the snow, the roads are getting slippery, too."

"We will let Susan tell you all about her adventure after we eat and warm up with some hot chicken noodle soup. She can also tell you what she learned tonight. You did learn something, I hope?"

"Yes, Mommy. I learned never to leave the house without asking 'mission first, so Mommy and Daddy will not worry 'bout me 'cause I am too little."

"Yes," I said.

"So where did you find her?" asked Margaret.

"Would you believe she was at the manger? She put Kevin in the manger so there would be a real baby there pretending to be Jesus. We didn't know whether to cry or scream when we saw them," I said. "I told her no one can take the place of Jesus. I told her the doll is there because it is too cold for a real baby."

"Well, our prayers were answered; they were both fine and just cold," said Margaret.

I think our hearts were still pounding, but thank goodness they were alright.

"Can I put the star on the tree since Kevin is asleep?" asked Andrew. "Ok, partner," Howard said, and he lifted Andrew up to reach the top of the tree. Susan showed Grand-mom baby Jesus in the manger and told her she was very gentle when she placed him there.

Howard and I took a few minutes together to discuss Susan's punishment.

"Susan, we know tomorrow is Christmas, but what you did was wrong. We have decided that you can spend the day as usual opening presents and enjoying dinner with everyone, but you cannot play with any of your new toys until the next day."

"What? But it's Christmas!" shouted Susan.

"You already have plenty of nice things to play with," Howard told her. "So on Christmas day after you open your presents you will place them back under the tree until the next morning."

"But, Daddy..." She started to cry.

Howard looked at her lovingly but sternly, and said, "I do not want to hear any crying about it. You will open them on Christmas and play with them the next day. Either you obey, or you open them and go to your room until bedtime. If you do not obey, we can make you wait until New Year's Eve."

"Yes, Daddy," Susan said. She barely whispered.

"Let us light the Advent candles," Katie called out. We all stood and watched as Katie carefully lit the four purple candles, and then she lit the large white candle in the center, which represents the birth of Jesus. We all softly sang "Silent Night" together. It was a peaceful moment.

We read the story about St. Nick and part of the Christmas story, but we were all just too tired to read any more. "Part two will be read tomorrow night," I said.

"How about Mom-Mom tells her little Christmas story, and then you will all go to bed? Come on, let's gather together," I said.

Margaret watched as our three older children settled down, and then she began to tell her story. "Did you know that some children do not believe in Santa Claus? They say you see him before Christmas everywhere, but how can so many Santas be the one and only Santa? I have seen him, too, before Christmas, but I have never seen him with his sleigh on the roof or go down a chimney. Some houses may not have chimneys, so I am sure he must get in another way.

"Many years ago, Santa was called by many different names. He was called Saint Nicholas and Father Christmas. He walked through the towns in Europe on Christmas Eve and delivered gifts to the children. He was very much a real person. Today we call him Santa Claus. We do not see the air, but we know it is there and we are breathing it. If Santa was not real for children, there would be no magic, anticipation, or excitement on Christmas Eve. A thousand years from now Santa will make glad the hearts of children. The magic of Santa will go on forever. Now it's time for bed, children; I love you, and sweet dreams," said Margaret.

The stockings were hung and the milk, cookies, and carrots were placed by the fireplace for Santa and the reindeer—actually the dog and the cat. Then it was off to bed. The children quickly fell asleep. Katie was already on the phone with her friends. "Katie, keep it short. It is time for bed, and Santa will be here soon," I whispered when I put my head in her door to say goodnight. Margaret was close behind me.

Katie hung up the phone and said, "I think I hear sleigh bells; listen!"

"Smarty pants," I said, and I went over to her bed to give her a kiss goodnight. Margaret did the same.

"Sweet dreams, girl," said Margaret.

"Goodnight, Mom...Grand-mom. See you on Christmas morning!" Katie said.

We were exhausted. It had been a busy day preparing for tomorrow, and this evening's ordeal with Susan had sapped the last of our energy. As I got ready for bed, I hoped that each of us had prepared our hearts for Jesus. We had been blessed again this evening, and all our children were safe at home.

I have been told that if God takes you to it, he will see you through it, as he did this evening. Prepare your heart for Jesus.

After the gifts were under the tree, Howard and I sat quietly with Dad, Jeanette, and Margaret remembering Christmases past and noting how quickly the children had grown. We sat with just the tree lights on, and some lighted decorations and a few candles. We talked about our mother and Howard's father. We shed some tears remembering the love we have for these family members who were no longer with us. It was a time of peace, hope, joy, and love. Yes, in our hearts and homes, we welcomed the King of Kings, *Jesus*. We prayed together with thanksgiving.

At one point, Dad said, "You still are using those old reflectors and the big lights. I remember you and your sister moving the light bulbs around so no two of the same color would be near each other."

"I have to admit, the larger bulbs really do light up the tree and the room," I said. "Also, they make us have good memories of Christmases past. Mother loved the Christmas season. We talked about getting a tree for next year with the lights already on it. We will see. I have to admit I will probably miss the brighter lights and the antique reflectors. Remember all the brandy, or was it whiskey, she poured over that fruitcake she made every year? You could almost get drunk from smelling it. That was Grand-mom's old recipe."

"I remember your mother was always the first one awake on Christmas morning," said Dad. "She would already be working on the turkey for dinner and would have special treats for breakfast that day. She would have donuts, a breakfast casserole, and a fruit salad prepared. She would have the candy and all the homemade cookies made and ready to be eaten. She really enjoyed the Christmas holidays."

"Mom, I remember Dad putting the Santa and sleigh in the front yard, and it was never just right, so you two would argue until you both had it just the way you wanted it," said Howard.

"I think your dad was as excited about Christmas as you were," smiled Margaret. "Each year he could not wait to take you to see Santa Claus, and he always made sure you received the toys you asked Santa for."

Jeanette chimed in and said, "I went downstairs to see the wreaths you and Katie made. Are you going to sell them in the covered bridge store?"

"We hope to," I said. "We sold a lot at the church bazaar, but that profit went to the church."

"Maybe I will buy some from you for the upcoming holidays," said Jeanette.

"No, you won't," I said. "You can have what you like. I won't let you buy them!"

"I would like the Valentine's Day wreath and the St. Patrick's Day wreath, then," said Jeanette. "The Valentine one is beautiful."

"Katie and I both worked on the Valentine one, and Katie made the St. Patrick's Day wreath."

"Do they take you long to make?" asked Jeanette.

"No, we can usually make two in an evening. Just make a note so you don't forget them when you leave," I told her.

"Kim made a beautiful nativity wreath for my front door," said Margaret. "Well, actually, it is the Holy Family. She put wooden rails on it to make it look like a stable. At times, I wonder if Jesus was born in a stable or a cave. Some say the stable was really a cave. I think I will stick with the thought of the stable or barn. Some say the tomb where Jesus was laid was actually a cave with a stone rolled in front of it."

"We will have to do some Bible studying," I said. "Luke calls it a manger, not a barn, stable, or cave. Now concerning his death, Matthew 27 says that Jesus was placed in a tomb cut out of a rock and a large stone was rolled in front of the entrance. People could walk in and out of the tomb after the stone was rolled away. Mark, Luke, and John are very much the same. So yes, the tomb definitely sounds like a cave."

Immanuel—God is with us.

CHAPTER 16

Christmas morning always comes too quickly. When I walk downstairs, the house is still quiet. I am sure it will not be for long. The sun is shining through the stained glass panel of the bay window producing a prism of colors. It has stopped snowing. The sun glistens on the snow-covered ground. The trees are beautiful as they sparkle with snowflakes. It is definitely a winter wonderland.

I did not sleep much, so I am sure I will welcome going to bed tonight. I awoke first so I would have time to make coffee, put on the tree lights, let out the dog, and feed both animals.

It wasn't long until I heard Andrew yelling, "It's Christmas! Wake up, everyone, wake up!"

Jeanette peeked around the kitchen door and said, "I smell the heavenly aroma of coffee, cinnamon coffee cake, and pumpkin muffins."

"Merry Christmas, Sis. I am so glad you and Dad are here," I whispered as she kissed my cheek.

"You know Dad is getting the baby. I bet he got little sleep waiting to get Kevin up for his first Christmas morning," Jeanette said with a chuckle.

"Dad was that way with all the children, and since Kevin is his last grandson, he wants to enjoy his first Christmas with him."

"Well, it sounds like thunder now!" In reality, it was Andrew and Susan running down the stairs.

This is the best part; we are all together as a family—a family that loves, respects, and cares for one another. Eating breakfast and opening presents take up most of the morning. Margaret and Dad are enjoying this time with their grandchildren. They are laughing at little Kevin especially. He is excited about everything, and as a typical little child, he likes the boxes and the dog and cat toys as much, or maybe even more, than his actual presents. He is crawling in and out of wrapping paper.

"I love watching the kids open their presents from Santa," said Jeanette. "They are so excited."

"Everyone make sure Kevin does not eat any of the ribbons or wrappings," I announced. Susan and Andrew are so loud and excited. Of course, Susan cannot wait to go to bed tonight so she can wake up and have it be tomorrow. Katie is trying on everything over her pajamas. Andrew cannot wait to go skiing.

"Wow!" screamed Andrew.

"Thanks, Andrew, I like the sweater," Katie said as she hugged her brother.

"Do you like your hair clips?" asked Susan. "Oh, yes," Katie said, and she gave Susan a kiss. "They look great with the sweater."

"Thanks, Susan," yelled Andrew.

"A karaoke machine—wow!" yelled Susan.

"That is yours, but I think we can all have fun with it," said Howard.

"Can we set it up now?" asked Susan.

"In a little while, after everyone opens their presents and we have had breakfast," Howard said. "Then again, you are still on punishment; we will talk about it later."

"We can't wait to see you ski, Andrew. I think you will like it," I said.

"I will take him after the holidays," Howard said. "Are you going to ski, too, Kim?"

"No, I will pass this time. I have not been skiing in so long I may hurt someone or myself. Maybe Katie will join you."

"Look, Dad, I have a Christmas hat for both the dog and the cat," said Andrew. "Do you think Kit-Kat will keep it on? Look, Dad, I think Midnight likes it. Dad, take a picture of me with the dog and the cat."

"After the holidays I would like to volunteer at the pet adoption center or deliver meals for seniors. Perhaps I can do something that will allow me to take Kevin with me. Babysitters are expensive," I said.

"You know if I am available, I would love to take care of Kevin," said Margaret.

"That would be great, Mom, and Kevin would like that, too," I said. "I know you enjoy your activities, and I don't want to take you away from them or your friends. I want to do something, but I have not made up my mind yet. I don't even know if I will have the time."

"My grandson will only be little for a short time, so I would rather enjoy my time with him," Margaret said.

The sounds of Christmas are wonderful. Opening the gifts from the little ones is always exciting. The gifts they buy from the Christmas store at school are so cute, especially if they wrapped the gifts themselves. Howard and I believe they must use a whole roll of tape on one gift. It is impossible to open one of their gifts without using scissors. Susan bought Howard one of those new gadgets advertised on the television. You can pop the little lights into the strings of Christmas lights automatically. It is amazing! I received a lovely necklace and earrings with purple stones. She knows I like the color purple.

"Mommy, you can wear the necklace and earrings with the new sweater Katie gave you. She showed the sweater to me first, and I kept a secret!"

"Wow, you kept a secret! That is wonderful, Susan," I said.

"Mommy, I am glad I do not have to keep the secret *no* more. It was hard." We all laughed.

Now it was time to pick up all the wrappings and find little Kevin!

"I have a question, Susan," I said. "How come Daddy got three presents and I only got two?"

"Mommy, I forgot I bought the tie tack and tie for him," she said.

"Come here, honey; I am just playing with you. You showed me the other gifts. Besides, I love the necklace and earrings, and yes, they do match the sweater Katie bought for me. I will wear them next Sunday to church."

"Goodie! I love you, Mommy," whispered Susan as she hugged me. I thought this was the best present.

"I love the camera, Kim," said Howard as he gave me a kiss.

"I knew you wanted one," I said. "Thank you for the mother's ring. I just love it; it is so beautiful. The six stones sparkle beautifully."

"I had a stone for each of our birthday months. Do you like the setting?"

"I love the setting," I said, and I threw a kiss in his direction.

"Kim and Howard, we love the family pictures," commented Dad and Jeanette.

"The photographer captured great shots, even with the dog and cat," said Margaret.

"Oh, my, was that a day. Thank goodness, she is a professional. We certainly had to be a challenge for her," I replied.

Dad noticed Kevin's antics and asked, "What is Kevin doing? He is pulling out all the clothes he got as presents and is putting them on his head. Where's that new camera, Howard?"

"Our little boy will never be this little again," Howard said, and he lifted Kevin into his arms and swirled him around to hear him giggle. "Here, Dad, do you want him?"

"Anytime, Howard, give me my grandson." Dad smiled and took Kevin into a bear hug.

"I forgot to tell you, Dad," I said. "We invited Benjamin Green to spend the day with us and have dinner here. He is a dear man. We know how much he misses his late wife, and this year he was not able to be with his son, daughter-in-law, and grandson for Christmas dinner. He lives close by, so it won't take long for them to return."

"Dad, would you like to take a short ride with me to pick up Benjamin Green?" Howard asked.

"Sure, that would be nice. I am sure I can use a breath of fresh air," answered Dad. "I believe I met him and his wife when you first moved up here."

"Maybe you did, Dad; I really do not remember," commented Howard.

⋆ ⋆ ⋆

"Hi, Mr. Green, Merry Christmas," everyone said in unison.

"Hi, everyone, Merry Christmas," said Mr. Green with a smile.

He brought a poinsettia plant for me, a bottle of wine for Howard, Bauer's General Store gift cards for the children, a stuffed Santa for Kevin, and a large box of candy from the Candy Cupboard for everyone.

"Mr. Green, you did not have to bring gifts for us. We are just so glad that you could join us for dinner and spend the evening with us," I said.

"That was the least I could do," Ben said, and he smiled warmly. "You are packaging food to go to my son's house, too."

"Oh, that is no problem. I made plenty so everyone could take some home. Mom and my sister were so much help."

"I telephoned my son to tell them I will enjoy another meal soon when Howard takes me to visit them. They both should be coming home soon. It has been a lot of stress on my daughter-in-law."

"Here, Uncle Ben," said Andrew. "We have a couple gifts for you, too."

We gave Mr. Green a subscription to *Reminisce* magazine, a magazine that is all about the days of yesteryear. Howard also bought him a nice cardigan V-neck sweater with buttons down the front.

"Oh, my goodness, you didn't have to get me anything," he said.

"We wanted to, Mr. Green. You are our guest. Merry Christmas!" I said.

"I really enjoy looking through the *Reminisce* magazines," said Dad. "I think they're written just for us old geezers!" Dad laughed.

"By the way, you can call me Ben or Benjamin."

"Ok, Benjamin, we certainly will."

"The children have always called you Uncle Ben or Uncle Benjamin," I said.

"Thank you, Uncle Ben and Uncle Benjamin!" the children shouted.

"I mean you and Howard, too, Kim," said Ben. "You both can call me Ben, too."

"It seems weird because I have called you Mr. Green for so long."

Susan looked adorable in the red dress my sister bought for her. The white furry collar and cuffs really set it off. She looked like a little princess. "Sis, I love her dress. I wish it came in my size. When I was a little girl, I always wanted a red Christmas dress like the ones that Rosemary Clooney and Vera Ellen wore in *White Christmas*. They were so beautiful and elegant," I said.

"Daddy, if I put on my tiara, will you take my picture?" asked Susan.

"If I take your picture, will it break my new camera?" asked Howard.

"Oh, Daddy, no!" Susan laughed.

"How about you stand next to your Pop-Pop and little brother, and I will take a picture," Howard said.

"Ok, Daddy," Susan said, and she smiled for the camera. "Cheese!"

Then Kevin said, "Ma-ma-ma."

"Oh, I heard that—my Christmas present!" I laughed.

"Alright, before it gets too late, let's try out the karaoke machine. I want to sing and dance to some songs with my talented family," shouted Howard.

Jeanette and I were watching from the sofa, and the next thing we knew, Andrew, Katie, Howard, and Susan were belting out "Y—M—C—A" as they made the letters in the air with their arms. Next, they sang, "Respect," and there was Margaret strutting her stuff. We were almost on the floor with laugher.

"Ok, our turn; come on, Sis, here we go," I said. We put on the song "It's Raining Men."

Ben, Howard, and Dad were really cheering and clapping.

"Come on, Uncle Ben," Susan said as she pulled him from the chair. "Now you, Daddy, and Pop-Pop have to sing something."

"Oh, honey, I don't know the words or how to sing," he said. Little did he know that the machine had all the words and the music, so he had no excuse.

"Ok," Dad said, "what do I sing?"

"I know, Dad, how about 'God Bless America'? The three of you probably know some of that one, and you can read the rest and sing off the screen," I told them. When they started singing, we all joined in and sang with them.

"This is really fun," Jeanette said.

"Katie looks nice in her outfit, too, Jeanette," I said. "I told her the other kids were getting dress clothes, so she had to do the same. With her long legs, she looks very sleek in the slim dress and little bolero jacket. I like the color black with the beige trim."

"Katie is so pretty she would look nice in a canvas bag," said Jeanette. "I am glad that Andrew liked the sport coat. He does look sharp in it."

When it was time to eat, the table was full with food and people. We held hands around the table as Howard said grace:

Our most heavenly Father,
Thank you for your incredible gift,
Jesus.
Bless this food and the hands that prepared it,
Bless each one here and grant traveling mercies
To me as I take Benjamin home,
And to my Mom as she drives home, and when
Jeanette and Dad leave.
Make us ever mindful of the needs of others.
In Jesus's precious name,
Amen.

As I looked around the table, I could feel the love in the room. Love comes in many shapes, sizes, and colors, but our hearts are big enough to carry all that love. It is then up to us to give that love away.

Christmas is Love.

It came to us in the form of a baby, an infant so small,
But one day he would shed his blood and
Die for our sins, in our place.

The house was quiet now. The children were in bed and asleep, except for Katie. She was watching television and pretending not to be sleepy. Howard took Ben home. Mom left after dessert. She prefers not to drive much after dark. Dad went to bed early, commenting that the last two days had done him in, and that tomorrow would be a long drive home to New Jersey. Midnight was asleep in front of the fireplace. I think she was exhausted from the baby chasing after her all day. Kit-Kat was batting a bow around on the floor. He really seemed to be enjoying himself.

Jeanette and I had a cup of Christmas tea and relaxed. I tried to encourage her to stay another day or two, but she had friends to visit, and Dad was ready to head home. Being a schoolteacher, she knows so many people and has many friends. It is hard to catch up with Jeanette. She is either going shopping, having lunch with friends, going to a show, or planning a trip with other schoolteachers. I call her the social butterfly of the family.

"Since it snowed, will you and Dad do the sleigh ride with us tomorrow?" I asked her. "Howard asked Ben when he took him home, but he said that he has a doctor appointment in the morning. The sleigh rides near here open at nine o'clock in the morning."

"Oh, yes, we want to do that with you, and then we can come back for some lunch, and after that, Dad and I can start for home. I really want to leave no later than twelve-thirty in the afternoon. I assume the roads will be busy with traffic with everyone heading home the day after Christmas. I hope to be home no later than eight o'clock in the evening," said Jeanette.

"I will pack food for you and dad and put it in the small cooler," I said. "Don't forget the wreaths you wanted. How about we go get them now and put them in your car?"

"Good idea, Kim," said Jeanette.

As we walked to her car, Jeanette commented, "I think you have more than ten inches of snow, and is it cold. I am wondering how much snow we received in New Jersey; that is, if we got any snow."

⋆ ⋆ ⋆

I opened the family room curtains. The moon shining on the snow was lovely. It was so cold today that the snow did not drip off the trees. The trees cast shadows on the lawn. Jeanette came to the window. "It sure is pretty," she whispered. "Breathtaking. Oh, look, Kim, are those three deer I see over there in the moonlight near the trees?"

"Oh yes, how lovely to see them on Christmas night," I said. "That is another Christmas memory for you to have today. I love deer. I am so glad that you and dad drove up here to spend Christmas with us."

"Are you kidding? He could not wait to see the kids. It is all about the children."

Jeannette fell silent for a moment, taking in the moonlit scene, and then she said quietly, "You have it all, Sis. You have children who love you, a husband who adores you, wonderful friends, and this beautiful home."

"You and Dad have wonderful lives, too," I replied.

"Yes, we are all blessed," Jeanette said. "But I think you are a blessed woman, Kim," she added.

"Yes, I am," I replied, "but I give God all the praise for that."

Dear Lord, thank you.

Yes, I am a blessed woman to have a wonderful
husband, sister, parents, and this joyous family.
Thank you, Heavenly Father, for your
Incredible gift—

Jesus

May you feel the blessings of Christmas,
The hope of a new year,
The peace in your heart,
And the faith to believe in the love of a miracle.
Peace be with you,
And may you have abundant joy.

All scriptures are from the New International Version of the Holy Bible:

REFERENCES:

The Night Before Christmas, Clement Clark Moore, Google

Remember Yesterday is History, by Alice Morse, Google

Forrest Gump, Paramount Pictures, Tom Hanks

The Hiding Place, Corrie ten Boom and John and Elizabeth Sherrill, Chosen Books, 1971, Betsie, page 181, section one, paragraph ten